MW00571309

TORONTO
BEST
URBAN
STROLLS

Time to rediscover Toronto's
daily little pleasures!

Word
— of —
Mouth
Production

À Max et André, qui nous ont quittés trop tôt
alors que j'écrivais ce guide...

Word-of-Mouth Production
299 Booth Avenue, Toronto, Ontario M4M 2M7, Canada
(416) 462-0670, nathalie@torontourbangems.com
www.torontourbangems.com

🄾 torontourbangems
🄵 torontourbangems

Writing and photos: **Nathalie Prézeau**
Illustrations: **Johanne Pepin**
Design and layout: **Publisher Friendly Inc.** (416) 333-9512
Proofreading: **Kerstin McCutcheon, Julie Sabourin**
Printing: **Marquis Book Printing Inc.** (418) 246-5666
Sales: **Ampersand Inc.**
Distribution: **University of Toronto Press**

Honorary members of the author's exclusive Friends Whom I Exploit Shamelessly Club:
**Bernard Dionne, Christian Castel, Claire Marier, Dany Lahaie, Diane Goulet,
François Bergeron, François Paquin, Josée Duranleau, Josette Bouchard,
Julie Bonin, Julie Sabourin, Kerstin McCutcheon, Laurent Bergeron,
Léa-Valérie Létourneau, Martine Côté, Martine Rheault, Monique Dobson,
Pascale Chapdelaine, Roxane Bergeron, Yannick Lallemant**

Library and Archives Canada Cataloguing in Publication

Title: Toronto best urban strolls / Nathalie Prézeau.
Names: Prézeau, Nathalie, 1960- author.
Description: Includes index.

Identifiers: Canadiana 2020020629X | ISBN 9780995064317 (softcover)
Subjects: LCSH: Toronto (Ont.)—Tours. | LCSH: Walking—Ontario—Toronto—Guidebooks. | LCSH: Toronto
(Ont.)—Guidebooks. | LCGFT: Guidebooks.
Classification: LCC FC3097.18 .P73 2020 | DDC 917.13/541045—dc23

It takes a village...

As you flip throught this book, I'm hoping that you feel what a labour of love it is.

Each circuit in this guide was explored over the course of four to six visits. Its photos, carefully selected from hundreds.

As I am writing these words, I'm marvelling at the road travelled since my first guide. Clearly, the writing of a worthy guide requires hard work, a good eye and strong perseverance, but sheer luck also played such an enormous part!

First of all, I was so lucky to have the opportunity to move to Toronto from Montreal. Over the years, I have thoroughly enjoyed my wonderful adopted city with the mindset of a traveller, never taking it for granted.

I was lucky that François, my husband, mastered InDesign. From the get go, I had help bringing my vision to life. He's done the templates for all my guides and I'm proud to say that we've worked all those years without a fight (except for that time when I hit him on the head with a dictionary... my bad!!!).

I was also lucky to have met my illustrator Johanne, way back when she was creating cool posters for a disco bar where I worked as a student. I then vowed that I would use her talents one day. She's done the covers of all my guides.

I was very lucky to meet Kerstin in my mothers' group, a girl whose job was copywriting. She ended up proofreading all my guides, making sure I didn't embarass myself too much when using my second language.

Finally, what good luck for me that you came upon this guide. I'm so happy my book found a good home in your welcoming hands. Enjoy!

With warmest regards,

Nathalie Prezeau

Nathalie Prézeau
Author, publisher, photographer
nathalie@torontourbangems.com

3

TORONTO BEST URBAN STROLLS **MAP**

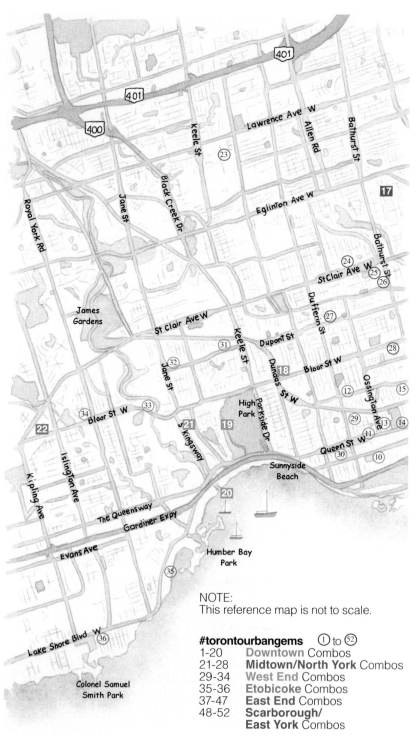

NOTE:
This reference map is not to scale.

#torontourbangems   ① to ㊿
1-20   **Downtown** Combos
21-28   **Midtown/North York** Combos
29-34   **West End** Combos
35-36   **Etobicoke** Combos
37-47   **East End** Combos
48-52   **Scarborough/
East York** Combos

TORONTO BEST URBAN STROLLS **MAP**

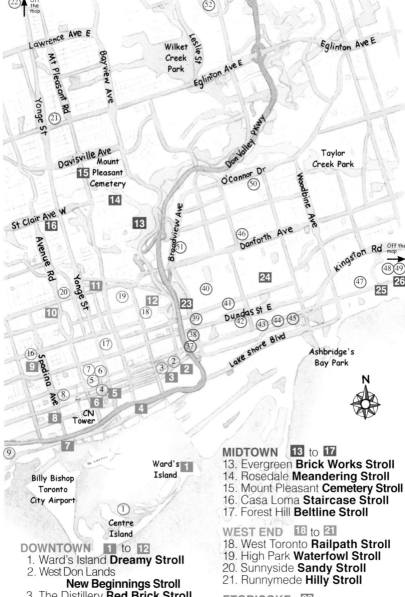

MIDTOWN `13` to `17`
13. Evergreen **Brick Works Stroll**
14. Rosedale **Meandering Stroll**
15. Mount Pleasant **Cemetery Stroll**
16. Casa Loma **Staircase Stroll**
17. Forest Hill **Beltline Stroll**

WEST END `18` to `21`
18. West Toronto **Railpath Stroll**
19. High Park **Waterfowl Stroll**
20. Sunnyside **Sandy Stroll**
21. Runnymede **Hilly Stroll**

ETOBICOKE `22`
22. Village of Islington **Murals Stroll**

EAST END `23` to `25`
23. Riverdale **Sunset Stroll**
24. Little India **Bohemian Stroll**
25. The Beach **Soothing Stroll**

SCARBOROUGH `26`
26. Scarborough **Cliffside Stroll**

DOWNTOWN `1` to `12`
1. Ward's Island **Dreamy Stroll**
2. West Don Lands
        New Beginnings Stroll
3. The Distillery **Red Brick Stroll**
4. East Bayfront **Waterfront Stroll**
5. Downtown **Courtyard Stroll**
6. The Path **Underground Stroll**
7. Queens Quay **Harbourfront Stroll**
8. Portland **Utterly Urban Stroll**
9. Kensington/Chinatown **Eclectic Stroll**
10. U of T **Ivy League Stroll**
11. Church **Village and Valley Stroll**
12. Cabbagetown **Victorian Stroll**

5

TORONTO BEST URBAN STROLLS

ETOBICOKE

EAST END

SCARBOROUGH

WHIMSICAL COMBOS WITH #torontourbangems

WARD'S ISLAND
DREAMY STROLL
1

Urban cottager

As you walk along the carless streets of the most intriguing neighbourhood in Toronto, you'll start to wonder how it would feel to leave the big city behind after a day's work and return to the cocoon of your cottage-like home on **Toronto Islands**. Most visitors stick to **Ward's** but there are more residences to be seen on adjacent **Algonquin Island**. The secluded boardwalk on the south shore overlooks the expanse of glistening water. Enjoy a glass of wine on the patio of nearby **The Riviera** and your experience of an urban cottager's lifestyle is complete.

STROLL
1

Toronto area
DOWNTOWN

Neighbourhood
Toronto Islands

Full loop
5.3 km (8,155 steps)

Time estimate
1 hr 20 min

Mindset
When you are craving connection with a source of awe.

Subway & TTC
• At **Union Subway Station**, catch **509** Harbourfront or **510** Spadina streetcars, on the underground platform, to Queens Quay Ferry Docks Terminal, 1-min walk from ferry.
• Streetcars **509**, **510**; buses **6**, **72**, **97**.

Best parking
• Go on **Best Parking app** (www.bestparking.com) and search **Jack Layton Ferry Terminal**.

Nathalie's TIPS
• See p. 15 for more tips to help you plan this walk.

First things first
This stroll starts with a ferry ride from the **Jack Layton Ferry Terminal** at the foot of Bay St. (Make sure you catch the **Ward's Ferry**.)

1 The little beach straight off the ferry is a favourite spot to watch the sunset.

2 Walk to the **Willow Square**, past the **Island Café** (good spot to grab coffee and a bite!) to admire the lovely *Pebble Mosaic,* a community project.

Channel Avenue
Then go east on Channel Ave to start your tour of the residential section. (Try to imagine this place back in the 1890's, when Torontonians came to pitch a tent on their rented summer spot!)

3 Turn left on 4th St. At the turn into 3rd St, you can see one of the only large and modern houses. The others are cottage-like.

4 Turn left again on Channel Ave and right on 1st St (peeking through every lane along the way). It is funny to see signs for streets and avenues in this carless environment.

5 Walk west on Lakeshore Ave, with one last turn right into 3rd St and around to 4th St. The streets are utterly charming, framed by all the greenery.

The Islanders have been renovating big time in the last few years. Property envy guaranteed! (A Residential Committee Trust waitlists potential buyers.)

6 The boardwalk starts by **Ward's Beach**. Strolling along, with such an endless horizon to our left, is so soothing!

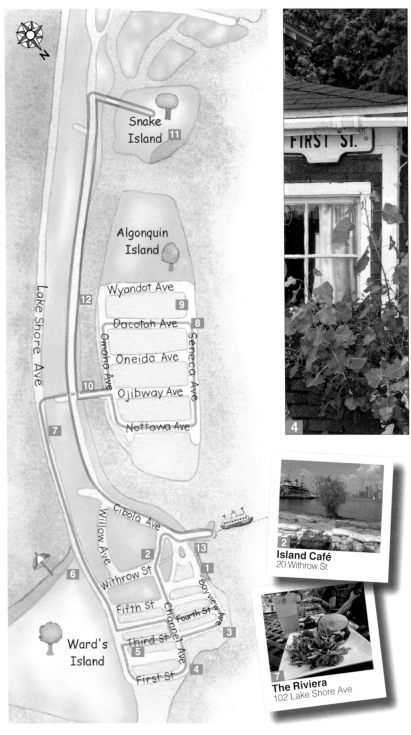

Snake Island 11

Algonquin Island

Wyandot Ave 9

Dacotah Ave 8

Oneida Ave

Ojibway Ave

Nottowa Ave

Omaha Ave

Seneca Ave

12

10

Lake Shore Ave

7

Cibola Ave

Willow Ave

Withrow St

Fifth St

Third St

First St

Channel Ave

Fourth St

Bayview Ave

2

13

1

5

3

4

6

Ward's Island

FIRST ST.

4

Island Café
20 Withrow St

2

The Riviera
102 Lake Shore Ave

7

7 Further west, you'll find **The Riviera - Ward's Island Kitchen** (formerly the **Rectory Café**) where you will be tempted to stop right away but don't worry, you'll be back!

Walking to the end of the boardwalk and back would add 30 minutes to your stroll. (Your call, but make sure you have time to catch your ferry ride back.)

Instead, I suggest you take the lane just west of the restaurant and cross over the pedestrian bridge to **Algonquin Island**.

Algonquin Island

By the bridge, a trading cart where residents drop off what they don't use and take what they need always makes me long for a more simple life...

It is quite entertaining to notice all the little details revealing what it must be like to live here. We saw people on bikes carrying huge balls. (They were heading to their gym class in the local community centre on Wyandot Ave.)

8 Turn left on Omaha Ave (you'll walk past a great tree house), then turn right on Dacotah Ave, where you'll see the **CN Tower** pointing at the end of the street.

9 Don't miss the post-card perfect white and blue cottage on your left on Seneca Ave.

It is a good spot to be reminded that in 1938, thirty houses were floated (yep, you read right!) from **Hanlan's Point** to **Algon-**

quin Island, to make room for the island airport. It was just the beginning.

In those days, the island's community extended from **Ward's Island** to **Hanlan's Point**. (Starting in the 1930's, people were allowed to build cottages on tent sites.)

By the 1950's, the **Toronto Islands** included 630 cottages or houses, a movie theatre, a bowling alley, stores, hotels, and dance halls!

This all changed with the construction of the Gardiner Expressway. This reconfiguration was going to erase the recreational land along Toronto's waterfront.

Metropolitan Toronto Council initiated the gradual removal of the islands community to make way for a municipal park.

By 1970, there were only 250 homes left on **Ward's** and **Algonquin Islands**, and the Islanders fought dearly, with the support of Torontotonians, to maintain the residential section we can all admire today.

10 Back to the walk. Going east on Seneca Ave, turn right on Nottawa Ave, and across the bridge.

By the way, July 28th is the "Day of the Bridge". In 1980, ready to fight back the threats of eviction, the residents (with the help of an elaborate system involving call chains and a World War 1 siren!) were warned of the arrival of the Sheriff and all gathered there to block his way.

Going right on Cibola Ave, you'll reach the bridge to **Snake Island**.

Snake Island

11 From the bridge, you can see a secluded swampy beach by the canal. Straight ahead is a trail leading to the north side of the Island, facing downtown Toronto.

If you turned right on Cibola Ave and took the right fork, you would get to the tiny **St. Andrew's by the Lake Church** in 10 minutes.

12 Walking back towards the ferry on Cibola Ave, you should be able to glimpse a few cool boat houses moored in the canal.

For a big finish, plan some time to stop at the funky **Island Café** on your right for great food, drinks, ice cream and island ambiance. Or, if you're in no rush, you could return to **The Riviera** by the boardwalk.

13 **Ward's Island Ferry** doesn't get as crowded as **Centre Island Ferry**, which is good news after a long walk. In addition, it is the only one of the three ferry lines operating off-season, from late October to early April.

NATHALIE'S **TIPS TO PLAN** THIS STROLL

For a shorter walk

The **Ward's** stroll between #1 and #7, and back to the ferry following Cibola Ave is my favourite section. It is 2.4 km long (a 40-min walk) and it is the location of the original camping lots erected in the the late 1800s. A good spot to wait for your friends who want to do the full loop is the lovely patio of **The Riviera Kitchen**.

About timing and logistics

• Note the **Ward's Ferry's** schedule to plan your way back. It could be one hour between ferries. Preferably buy your ticket online to avoid the longer line-up. Search *Toronto Island Park* on **www.toronto.ca** for the schedules and to buy tickets. Cost for return trip including tax: $9.25/adult, $4.40/child.

• I've visited **Ward's Island** in winter during a snow flurry and it was beautiful. Even better if **The Riviera** is open, which may be only on Sundays during the winter. Check with them at **www.islandriviera.com**.

• The month of May has seen floods in recent years. They are getting better at managing the water levels but parts of the **Islands**, such as Snake Island or sections of the amusement park, might be closed.

Romantic mood

• Catching a water taxi ride to **Toronto Islands** is a nice indulgence on a romantic date. You can catch one at the pier at the foot of York St, on the east side of **Queens' Quay Terminal** ($10 per person for a one-way).

• Maybe not for a first date but **Hanlan's Beach** is the only "clothing optional" beach in Toronto.

• Have a drink and dance to a live band with a view over the cityscape at **The Upper Deck** (see #torontourbangem #1 on p. 218).

• **Ward's Island Ferry** deck is not as crowded as **Centre Island**'s. The small beach nearby is the perfect spot to watch the sunset as the sky takes on dreamy pastel hues.

Family fun

• The **Centre Island Ferry** will take you the closest to the family attractions: **Centreville Amusement Park**, **Toronto Boat Rentals** (for paddleboat, kayak & canoe rentals), **Franklin Children's Garden**, playground, **Centre Island** beach and belvedere. Search *Toronto Island Park* on **www.toronto.ca** for details.

• I can't recommend enough renting a 2 or 4-seater at the **Island Bicycle Rental** for your family (**www.torontoislandbicyclerental.com**). Big success with teens!

A little extra in the area

• Check the mini-walk #1 on page 218 in the last chapter **#torontourbangems**.

WEST DON LANDS
NEW BEGINNINGS STROLL
2

Good on so many levels

To **Waterfront Toronto**, the entity funded by the federal, provincial and municipal governments to oversee all aspects of the planning and development of Toronto's central waterfront, it is clear that parks are critical to the development of new neighbourhoods. The beautiful integration of quality design, landscape architecture, public spaces and public art in and around **Corktown Common** is the best example of what happens when the three levels of government play nicely, and are able to present a strong and unified vision to their partners and developers.

STROLL
2

Toronto area
DOWNTOWN

Neighbourhood
**West Don Lands
+ Corktown**

Full loop
3.5 km (5,385 steps)

Time estimate
55 minutes

Mindset
When you want to rekindle your faith in Toronto's ability to come up with stellar urban development.

Subway & TTC
• Streetcars **501**, **504**.

Best parking
• Go on **Best Parking app** (www.bestparking.com) and search **The Distillery District**.
• If you don't find street parking, go to the paid parking lot of The Distillery (entrance on Parliament).

Nathalie's TIPS
• See p. 23 for more tips to help you plan this walk.

Post Pan-Am

This is a fantastic walk, thanks to the sustainable development catalyzed by the **Toronto Pan Am Games 2015**, which left behind the **Cooper Koo Family YMCA**, a beautified skatepark, a new section of Front St filled with art pieces, and a natural link between **The Distillery** and **Riverside** neighbourhoods.

First things first

1 Even if you don't want to start this walk with tea or coffee, go inside **Odin Café and Bar** to see the slick decor (check that ceiling!).

Notice the cross over one of Odin's eyes on the logo at the door and wolf mural inside. They are references to the facts that Odin had two wolf companions and that he sacrificed one of his eyes to acquire cosmic knowledge.

2 Walk eastbound on King St E to the **Queen Street Bridge** going over the **Don River**. On its top you can read the caption: *The river I step in is not the river I stand in.* They are wise words from philosopher Heraclitus chosen by artist Eldon Garnet. What they mean is open for discussion. (His contemporaries called him The Obscure.)

The very good Italian restaurant across the bridge is aptly named **Il Ponte** (625 Queen St E). It features the landmark bridge on its walls, and so does **Blackbird Baking Co.** recently opened a bit further down (635 Queen St E).

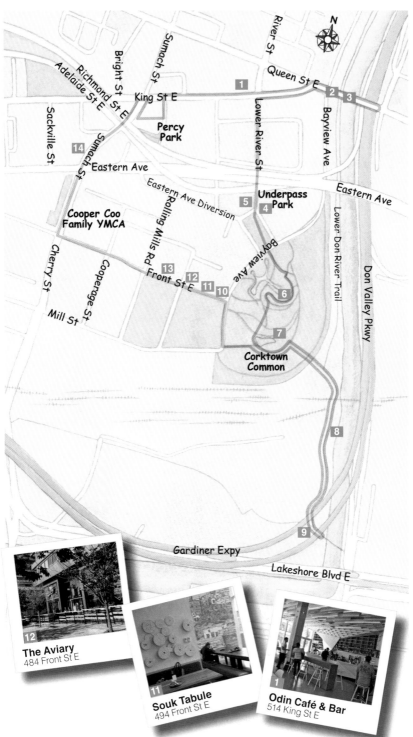

The Aviary
484 Front St E

Souk Tabule
494 Front St E

Odin Café & Bar
514 King St E

3 Looking west from the bridge, you get a good view of the man-made hill serving as a flood protection landform. This is what allowed this industrial site to turn into a mixed-use residential area.

The park, skatepark and public art are all nicely lit at night, thanks to great urban planning.

Underpass Skatepark

On your way back to King St E, walk left on Lower River St until you reach Toronto's most beautiful skatepark. In light of the **Pan-Am Games 2015**, a major budget was allocated to commission artists to adorn all the underpass pillars.

4 It is now a popular hub for skaters and basketball players, families enjoying the modern playground and passersby on their way to **Corktown Common**. At night, lights on the pillars add an architectural dimension.

5 This location is now home to the charming **Underpass Farmers Market** on Thursdays, 3 to 7 pm, late May to early October.

Corktown Common

Continue southbound on Lower Jarvis St, to the park's entrance at the foot of the **Lawren Harris Square**, off Bayview Ave. If you take the right fork, you'll see the wetland pond, home to happy frogs.

I like to take the left one and go up the first stairs, then the next left fork, to reach the highest point of the hill (a secluded little nook).

6 After the next turn, you can take the stairs down towards the elegant pavilion.

7 The beautiful splash pad by the pavilion is fit with big river boulders and overlooks downtown.

8 Walk east behind the pavilion to take the stairs down towards the **Don River**. On the other side of the tunnel, turn right into the **Lower Don River Trail**. Be careful! You are sharing the path with speedy cyclists.

9 More amazing water themed murals await on the pillars, part of the *Love Letter Projects* to bring awareness towards fresh water protection. Return to the pavilion and go down to Mill St on the west side.

10 The **Front Street Promenade** features major public art commissioned by **Waterfront Toronto**, starting with the whimsical *Garden of Future Follies*, near the excellent **Souk Tabule** and **The Aviary**, which stays open late! (Polaroids **#11** and **#12** on map.)

13 The blue *Water Guardians* are already quite a sight. It's even better 2 to 4 hours after sunrise, when the sun rays play with the panels on the nearby building!

Pass the **Dark Horse Espresso Bar**, cross Cherry St and walk northbound.

14 You will find a spectacular cut-out artwork on Sumach St. Further at King St E, look west to admire the four giants on pillars, by street artist trio Shalack Attack.

Then cross Sumach St and return southbound to reach **Percy Park**. It opens into one of the few private streets in the city.

NATHALIE'S **TIPS TO PLAN** THIS STROLL

For a shorter walk

In order to shorten this stroll to a 2.3-km loop (35-min walk), simply skip #8 and #9. When you reach the splash pad at #7, walk down the hill, turn right at Bayview Ave and left onto Front St E. Follow #10 to #14 but once you've admired the artwork on Sumach St, continue eastbound on Eastern Ave, follow the paved path leading back to the colourful pillars of the **Underpass Skatepark** and return back to your starting point on King St E.

About timing and logistics

• **Corktown Common** is one of the four locations featuring outdoor movie nights organized in summertime by the **Toronto Outdoor Picture Show (TOPS)**. For the occasion, a large screen is installed down the hill hidden behind the bush, just south of the pavilion and the playground. Consult their programming on **www.topictureshow.com**.

• The **Underpass Park Farmers Market** is open on Thursdays from 4 pm to 7:30 pm (on the west side of Lower River St). Located amidst the murals, it is one of the prettiest settings in Toronto for such a market (see #5). Expect live music. See **www.facebook.com/Corktown.Marke**t for updates and to confirm the hours.

Romantic mood

• Consider the elegant and breezy **Il Ponte** serving classic Italian dishes in a cool location (it is right by the bridge on the east side of #2).

• Except for #7 and #8, the rest of this stroll is nicely lit, which makes it a lovely night walk. In addition, **The Aviary Brew Pub** (see #12) stays open quite late so you can end the walk with a nightcap. See **https://aviary brewpub.com** for details.

• There's also the new **Gusto 501** (501 King St E, 100 metres west of Sumach St) which opened in 2020. Its architecture is spectacular, inside out, with seating on four levels and a very promising rooftop. Visit **www. gusto501.com** to make reservations.

Family fun

• With the skatepark and basketball hoops on the east side and the modern playground on the other, parents can watch over their younger offspring while keeping an eye on the oldest enjoying the **Underpass Skatepark** (see #4).

• The splash pad is truly fantastic (see #7). I will never tire of the view. The original playground located east of it is large, with a sand pit and a fun slide.

A little extra in the area

• Check the mini-walk #2 on page 218 in the last chapter **#torontourbangems**.

THE DISTILLERY
RED BRICK STROLL
3

Modern Victorian

It was a stroke of genius to refurbish the Victorian industrial buildings left by the **Gooderham & Worts** empire into a beautiful historical haven. The four-block carless site includes condos, art galleries, one-of-a-kind retail shops and restaurants. It is peppered with huge pieces of art and outdoor patios to admire it all. Exposed brick everywhere makes you feel like you're in a European village. The **Flatiron Building**, where the distiller had its office further west, is the perfect complement to this stroll.

STROLL
3

Toronto area
DOWNTOWN

Neighbourhood
Distillery District
+ St. Lawrence

Full loop
3.5 km (5,385 steps)

Time estimate
55 minutes

Mindset
When you want to
time travel... but be
back for dinner.

Subway & TTC
• Streetcar **504**,
buses **65, 121, 365**.
• **King Subway Station** is a 3-min walk
from **Berczy Park**.

Best parking
• Go on **Best Parking app** (www.bestparking.com) and search
The Distillery District.

Nathalie's TIPS
• See p. 31 for more
tips to help you plan
this walk.

First things first

1 It is fun to enter **The Distillery** from Gristmill Lane (off Parliament St, just south of Mill Street), where you'll see a modern glass version of a "flatiron building" near the instagrammable giant heart.

2 **Arvo Coffee** on your right is a great meeting point. Their coffee is excellent and they have a toast menu. (Check their tiny monastic nook!)

The Distillery

This national historic site includes over forty red brick buildings proclaimed "the best preserved collection of Victorian industrial architecture in North America".

3 A bit further, past the giant spider-like sculpture, take a few minutes to explore the beautiful **Thomson Landry Gallery**, across from its sister gallery. Around the corner on your right, wearable masterpieces are beautifully showcased inside **Fluvog Shoes** store.

4 An alembic-like sculpture in the middle of the plaza is a clever reference to **The Distillery**'s history.

5 Another great café, **Balzac's**, is unique for its amazing chandelier and the tables in the mezzanine.

Down Case Good Lane is **Artscape Case Goods Warehouse** with artists studios inside.

Turn left to reach Tank House Lane, then right, for more shops to explore, such as **Bergo Designs**, a fantastic place for last-minute gifts, small or ambitious.

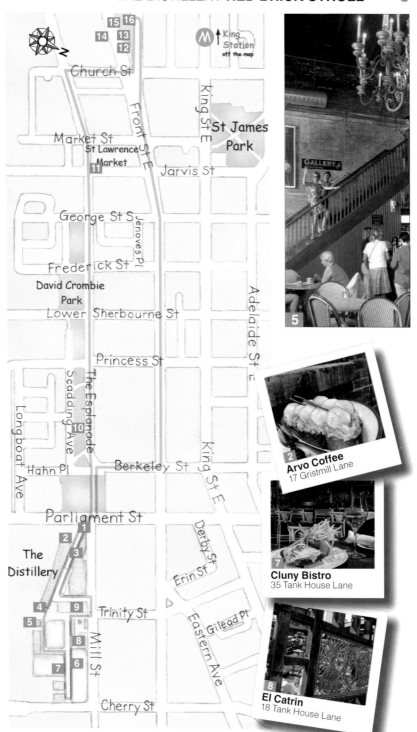

Arvo Coffee
17 Gristmill Lane

Cluny Bistro
35 Tank House Lane

El Catrin
18 Tank House Lane

6 Further, just before the **Young Centre for the Performing Arts**, is **SOMA Chocolate & Gelato**, one of the few artisanal shops in Toronto making its own chocolate from cocoa beans. Among my favourite treats: their thick and spicy hot chocolate (so soothing during a visit in the fall) and any of their dark chocolate truffles.

7 French music usually comes out of **Cluny Bistro and Boulangerie**'s speakers, inviting us inside to admire its gorgeous ceiling. They also have a lovely covered patio in summer time. But my favourite is the one at **El Catrin**!

8 Everything about Mexican **El Catrin** is artsy and whimsical: the outdoor lanterns and cut-out panels at the entrance, the giant lampshades, and the beautiful wall-to-ceiling mural inside, by Oscar Flores.

9 There's more shopping to be done along Trinity Street, the heart of **The Distillery**. It is welcoming year-round but especially pretty during the winter events (**Toronto's Christmas Market** and **Toronto Light Festival**).

Reach Mill St and turn left, then take the first lane on your left to see an interesting artifact in a showcase. There are many artifacts peppered all around the site but this one is the largest. Then continue back to Parliament St.

This walk is named the "red brick stroll" because the path linking Parliament St all the way to Jarvis St is lined with reddish brick.

The Esplanade

On your right, on Berkeley St, you'll see the **Canadian Stage Company**'s lovely red brick building (also hosting the **Théâtre français de Toronto**).

10 Through the 10-min walk along The Esplanade, in the **David Crombie Park**, there are murals, fountains, playgrounds, a wading pool and a garden.

Lower Jarvis Street

11 Where the red brick-lined sidewalk stops, the historic **St. Lawrence Market** takes over. Boasting over 120 merchants, it caters to Toronto foodies from Tuesday to Saturday.

Church Street

Keep strolling west on The Esplanade, past the cute little Market St. Beyond Church St, The Esplanade is elegant, with large patios on one side and **Novotel**'s chic Parisian arches on the other.

On the north/west corner of Church St and The Esplanade, look for the tiny street art by Banksy, protected by Plexiglas in the back of the **Goose Island Brewhouse**.

Front Street

12 At the corner of Front and Church is Toronto's historic landmark the **Flatiron Building**. (New York also has one but it was built AFTER Toronto's.) Its official name is the **Gooderham Building**, as in Gooderham & Worts distillery. It was built in 1892 and served as the distillers' offices for 60 years.

13 Make sure you check the back of the **Flatiron Building**.

14 It features a very cool trompe-l'oeil reproducing the building across Front St, currently home to **Winners**.

15 There's definitely a European vibe about this block facing the gorgeous public space at **Berczy Park**, especially since they've added the deceptively classic fountain (featuring over 20 cast-iron dogs... and one cat, plus another I spied on the premises, can you see it?).

16 I was thrilled by the added whimsy brought to this great park in 2017 with the two giant hands by Luis Jacob. Apparently, it was supposed to be a kids play structure, where the hands would hold a string game the kids could climb into. The installation was aptly named *Jacob's Ladder*. (Chuckles!)

The stretch going eastbound from this park to the **St. Lawrence Market** at Lower Jarvis St is lovely.

The small square by the **Market Lane Park** before Jarvis St hides the **Imagine Cinemas Market Square**, one of Toronto's most affordable movie theatre, offering $12 luxury recliner seating and $7 Tuesdays!

Keep walking east for a peek at one more red brick building: the imposing **Canadian Opera Company**, before turning right on Berkeley St to return to your starting point.

NATHALIE'S **TIPS TO PLAN** THIS STROLL

For a shorter walk
For a 2.1-km loop (30-min walk) including **The Distillery District** and a stroll along **David Crombie Park**, follow #1 to #10, and return.

About timing and logistics
• **King Subway Station** is a 4-min walk from #16 (in **Berczy Park**).
• I usually end up parking in the **Green P** parking lot at the foot of Church St.
• Did you know that **Théâtre français de Toronto** (Toronto's French Theatre) presents some of its French plays with English supertitles? A cool way to brush up on your French.
• You could combine this walk with a movie at the small **Imagine Cinemas Market Square** at 80 front St E, across from the **St Lawrence Market** (at #11). Their screens are small but tickets are cheaper than in big movie theatres and they have reclining seats! Check their calendar at **www.imaginecinemas.com**.

Romantic mood
• **Arvo Coffee** (see #2) has the tiniest room, wide enough for one big comfy leather chair and a side bench. The perfect little nook for two!
• In wintertime, bundle up and leisurely stroll around to enjoy the **Toronto Light Festival** throwing a warm glow over the red brick walls. Then go for a thick hot chocolate at **Soma** (see #6).
• In summertime, **Berczy Park** (see #15) feels like a Parisian public place, with its tables and chairs under the shady trees, overlooking the majestic fountain and surrounded by four-storey brick buildings.

Family fun
• Check inside the different historic buildings. They feature interesting distillery artifacts that should interest the small engineers.
• Everyone loves browsing at **Bergo Design** (across from #7). They carry many amusing trinkets in their many gadget sections, along with more expensive and beautifully designed gift ideas.
• Santa hangs around the **Toronto Christmas Market** at **The Distillery**, usually for one month prior to December 25. See **www.torontochristmasmarket.com** for updates.
• **David Crombie Park** (see #10) includes many fun amenities: a basketball court with heart mural, a large play structure, a wading pool with spraying arch and a secret garden.
• Water sprays are spurting out of the mouth of the fun dogs around the large public fountain in **Berczy Park**! Maybe bring an extra set of clothes?

A little extra in the area
• Check the mini-walks #2 on page 218 and #3 on page 219 in the last chapter **#torontourbangems**.

EAST BAYFRONT
WATERFRONT STROLL
4

Slick and shiny Toronto

There was a time when there were only a few incentives to drag us east of **Queen's Quay Terminal** such as the point zero of Ontario's longest street (Yonge St) marked with engraved brass letters on the sidewalk and **Redpath**'s whale mural. Then came **Sugar Beach** (with the pink umbrellas), followed by **Sherbourne Common** (with water sculptures and a canal redirecting treated water to the lake). Now, there's a gorgeous tree-lined waterfront promenade with huge patio and a cluster of breathtaking luxury condos with public art to admire.

STROLL
4

Toronto area
DOWNTOWN

Neighbourhood
East Bayfront

Full loop
4.2 km (6,462 steps)

Time estimate
1 hr 05 min

Mindset
When you feel like anchoring yourself in the 21st Century.

Subway & TTC
• Buses **6**, **72**, **75**.
• At **Union Subway Station**, look for the underground street-car to Queens Quay Ferry Docks Terminal.

Best parking
• Go on **Best Parking app** (www.bestpark-ing.com) and search **Sugar Beach**.

Nathalie's TIPS
• See p. 39 for more tips to help you plan this walk.

First things first

1 You can grab a **Star-bucks** coffee down-stairs at **Loblaws** and drink it by the windows on its third floor. Definite-ly a good meeting point, with a vantage point to admire the shimmering lake, **Sugar Beach**'s pink umbrellas and the whale mural on the facade of the **Redpath** refinery.

2 By the way, this mural is #70 in the *Whaling Wall* series of 100 murals done worldwide by art-ist Wyland from the 80's to 2008. We're lucky to have one in Toronto!

Sugar Beach

3 **Canada's Sugar Beach** was a most welcome addition in the area in 2010, with 36 per-manent pink umbrellas, beach chairs, white sand with tiny bits of quartz and a cute spray pad, which is lit at night. Note that it gives no access to the water.

The Promenade

4 Walk around the building to access the **Water's Edge Prome-nade**. It is paved with cob-blestones bearing a maple leaf pattern and lined with trees and designer bench-es. Over 10 years, the Maple trees have grown to form a stately alley provid-ing refreshing shade.

5 Make sure you get a good look inside the **Corus** building for the school of iridescent Neon Tetra fish swimming from the ceiling, and the 4-sto-rey-high flume slide for the employees. Very Pixar-ish.

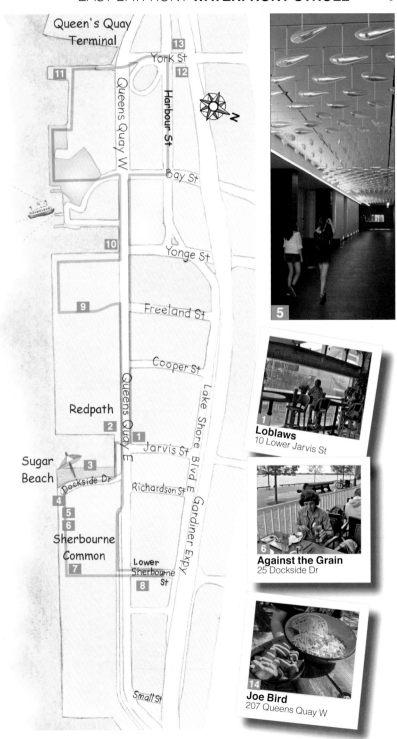

Loblaws
10 Lower Jarvis St

Against the Grain
25 Dockside Dr

Joe Bird
207 Queens Quay W

6 You'll notice the huge waterfront patio of **Against the Grain Urban Tavern**. The promenade is not as touristic as Harbourfront's, which makes it the perfect spot to have a relaxing cocktail. (Just saying.)

Sherbourne Common

7 Further east, past **George Brown College**, is the river-like canal of **Sherbourne Common**. This park, which spreads on both sides of Queens Quay, actually is a facility for the treatment of storm water, with modern playground as a bonus on the north side.

8 The shiny central building is not just an architectural statement, it filters and releases the water into the canal, thanks to three tall functional sculptures by Jill Anholt (turning into lovely blue veils at night).

You are now at the edge of what could have been the smart city project initiated by Google's **Sidewalk Labs** (cancelled in May 2020).

9 The luxurious condos will compete for your attention as you walk back along Queens Quays, but **Pier 27 Condos** definitely wins with its architectural masterpiece matched with equally breathtaking public art.

Walk down the paved path reaching another section of the **Water's Edge Promenade** between 39 and 29 Queens Quay, to admire the sculptures by Alice Aycock, including her splendid *Toronto Twister*.

Follow the promenade westbound and return to Queens Quay.

The next phase of revitalization is happening west of **Loblaws** to Yonge St, with most action taking place around One Yonge.

Yonge Street

10 At the foot of Yonge St, you'll see brass letters inlaid in the sidewalk, claiming this is Canada's longest street.

Harbour Square Park

The **Jack Layton Ferry Terminal**, allowing you to reach **Toronto Islands**, is just past the **Westin Harbour Castle**, at the foot of Bay St.

For years, I passed by the park to the west of the ferry ramp without checking it out, assuming it was just a little uninteresting patch of greenery. My bad! **Harbour Square Park** actually offers a lovely stroll along the waterfront and leads to **Queen's Quay Terminal**.

Waterfront Toronto has big ambitions for the eventual revitalization of this park and the ferry terminal. The winning design will double the size of the

terminal and give it an accessible green roof. How exciting? They will also sculpt the park's landscape and add play areas.

11 The western section of this park is called **Sundial Folly Park**, after the intriguing sphere done by John Fung and Paul Figueiredo in 1995 (still there at the time of print). Fun fact: One can whisper at one end of the sundial and be heard loud and clear on the other end.

12 Walk to **One York**, past Harbour St, and go in to marvel at the giant spiral by Mariko Mori. It you follow the **PATH** sign, you'll reach the famous *Guard with Balloon Dog* by Banksy, preserved and showcased by the developer.

13 The spectacular atrium at **10 York**, across York St, is also a statement to the waterfront's new vision.

Keep walking east on Harbour St, then right into Bay St, to get to the **Queens Quay Ferry Docks Terminal** one stop away from **Union Station**.

Queen's Quay Terminal

If you want to have a bite after lunch, I recommend walking down to **Queen's Quay Terminal**. There are plenty of restaurants with patios. I have enjoyed great meals, inside and out the whimsical **Joe Birds** (polaroid **#14** on map).

Closer to the starting point of this stroll, **Against the Grain Urban Tavern** offers a wide choice of fresh and well presented dishes.

NATHALIE'S **TIPS TO PLAN** THIS STROLL

For a shorter walk
This lovely 2.1-km loop (30-min walk) includes the newest improvements to the waterfront between **Sherbourne Common** water treatment system and the breathtaking *Twister* installation. Simply follow #1 to #9 and return along Queens Quay E.

About timing and logistics
• If you are considering visiting **Against the Grain Urban Tavern**, call them to check their current parking policy. They used to offer a parking discount to their customers: (647) 344-1562.
• The **Redpath Sugar Refinery** is pretty much at the heart of this stroll. It inspired the name of **Sugar Beach** (including the choice of its fine-grained quartz sand) and the artwork out of sugar inside the **Corus** building. It is still processing sugar from the Caribbean Islands and Brazil, hence the big cargo ships we often see by **Sugar Beach** from late March to end of November.

Romantic mood
• The public art is very nicely lit at night, all around **Sherbourne Common** (with the cityscape in the background) and the **Water's Edge Promenade** (with lights reflecting on the water). At night we can see a zigzag shape of lightning moving from the ceiling through **Corus**' glass facade. I highly recommend it! There's a parking lot on the north side of **George Brown College**.

Family fun
• The playground in **Sherbourne Common** north of Queens Quay E is quite modern. Leave it to the kids to find good use for all the sculpture-like structures. South of Queens Quay E, there's a splash pad which turns into a rink in wintertime.
• **Sugar Beach**'s cute little splash pad is irresistible. So are its inviting Muskoka chairs and wonderfully soft sand.
• **Cherry Beach** is the closest beach with water access. It is normally only 3 km from **Sugar Beach** (going eastbound on Queens Quay E to reach Lake Shore Blvd E and turning right onto Cherry St). There was construction at the time of print requiring you to take a detour. **Cherry Beach** is a long and narrow beach with a roomy off-leash dog park in the most natural setting.

A little extra in the area
• You could continue your walk west of **Harbourfront Centre** with the *Queens Quay HARBOURFRONT Stroll* (see page 56). • You could be at **The Distillery District** in 10 minutes if you continue east of #8 on Queens Quay E, which turns into Parliament St. See *The Distillery RED BRICK Stroll* on page 24.

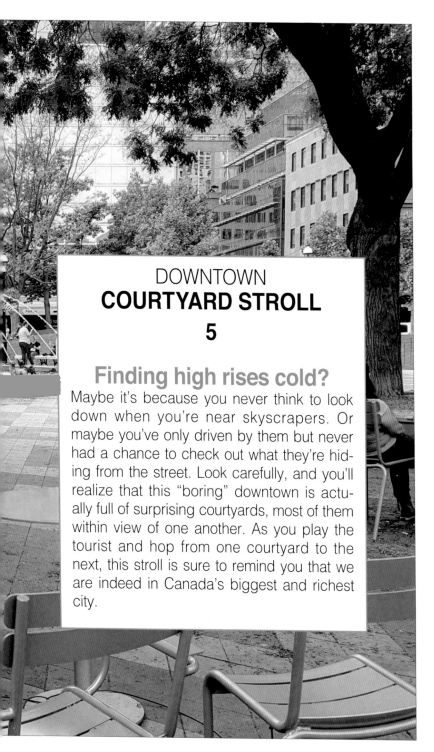

DOWNTOWN
COURTYARD STROLL
5

Finding high rises cold?

Maybe it's because you never think to look down when you're near skyscrapers. Or maybe you've only driven by them but never had a chance to check out what they're hiding from the street. Look carefully, and you'll realize that this "boring" downtown is actually full of surprising courtyards, most of them within view of one another. As you play the tourist and hop from one courtyard to the next, this stroll is sure to remind you that we are indeed in Canada's biggest and richest city.

STROLL
5

Toronto area
DOWNTOWN

Neighbourhood
**Financial District
+ Entertainment
District**

Full loop
4.6 km (7,075 steps)

Time estimate
1 hr 10 min

Mindset
When you want a
delightful surprise
at every turn.

Subway & TTC
• The walk starts at
King Subay Station
but you can also exit
at **St. Andrews**, or
Union Subway Stations.

Best parking
• Go on **Best Parking
app** (www.bestpark-
ing.com) and search
Union Subway Station.

Nathalie's TIPS
• See p. 47 for more
tips to help you plan
this walk.

First things first
1 I love to stop at
Dineen Coffee for
its French vibe, from the
old corner building and
patio to the high ceiling
and woodwork inside, to
the baristas' checkered
shirts. It is located two
blocks north of **King Subway Station**.

2 Choose the Italian
bakery **Sud Forno**,
across the street, for a
delectable breakfast. The
decor is wonderful and the
display counters, so ap-
petizing. (It opens at 7:30
am on weekdays, a bit
later on weekends.)

3 While you're on Temperance St, walk
past the building on your
right to see a large art installation.

The large artwork
gets even more interest-
ing when you learn that
each square represents
different trades in the
construction industry.

Normally, you would
have access to a water-
fall, walkways and the
Cloud Garden green-
house. (It is closed until
2022 to facilitate major
construction nearby.)

Adelaide St E
Walk south on Yonge St,
cross at Adelaide St, on
the south side, and go
eastbound on Adelaide
St E.

4 On your right, you
will see a chiseled
glass labyrinth leading
to a lovely courtyard with
an assortment of sculp-
tures with fountains.

South of the courtyard,
turn left on King St E.

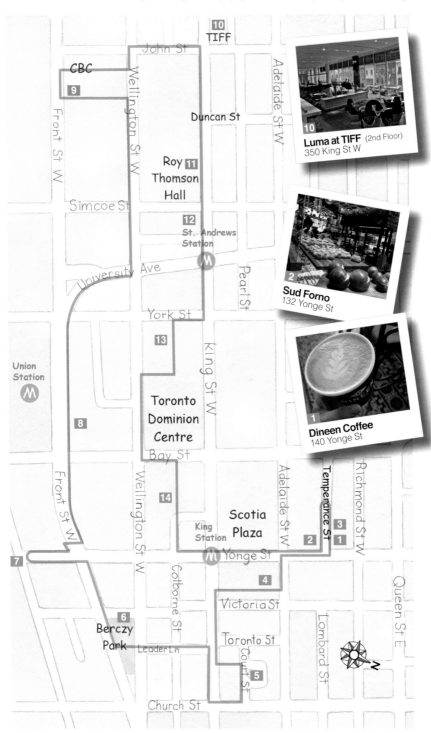

10 TIFF

John St

CBC

9

Front St W

Wellington St W

Adelaide St W

Duncan St

Luma at TIFF (2nd Floor)
350 King St W

Roy
Thomson
Hall **11**

Simcoe St

12
St. Andrews
Station Ⓜ

Sud Forno
132 Yonge St

University Ave

Pearl St

York St

13

King St W

Union
Station
Ⓜ

Dineen Coffee
140 Yonge St

Toronto
Dominion
Centre

Bay St

8

Wellington St W

14

Front St W

Richmond St W

Temperance St

Adelaide St W

3

2 **1**

King
Station
Ⓜ Yonge St

Scotia
Plaza

4

7

Colborne St

Victoria St

Toronto St

Lombard St

Queen St E

6
Berczy
Park

Leader Ln

Court St

5

Church St

N

43

Court Square

5 Walk into the alley you will notice past Toronto St. The path leads to Court St and the little **Court Square** with a granite platform with books (of law, one presumes), running fountain and a section of arches with benches, quite nice in the summer when covered with plants. It is adjacent to the inviting backyard patio of **Terroni**, which adds life to this quiet nook.

Front Street

At Church St, check the colourful mural on your left. Then turn right, cross King St E and walk west. Turn left on Leader Lane. You will pass the bright and cheerful **P.J. O'Brien Irish Pub**.

6 Straight ahead, it will lead you to **Berczy Park**. How many dogs can you count? And cats? There's an European feel to this beautiful park surrounded by old brick buildings. The trompe-l'oeil mural on the **Flatiron Building** reproduces the facade of nearby **Winners**.)

7 Walk westbound past the park and cross Front St E at the lights. Keep walking south on Yonge St and expect to be amazed by the impressive eagle on the **Backstage Condo** building at The Esplanade!

Back to Front St, cross at the lights to admire the historic **Hockey Hall of Fame**. As you walk further west, you will see the colourful art installation running inside the new **Chotto Matte** restaurant.

8 If walking on a weekday, go up the stairs by the colourful characters on the **Royal Bank Plaza** wall, to see if you can access the fantastic patio of **RBC** (closed in the winter).

Peek inside the revamped **Fairmont Royal York** to see the chic **Clockwork Champagne & Cocktails** lounge.

Continue north on University Ave. In summer, you'll see a gorgeous wall fountain simulating a stream along the first building on your right on University Ave.

Turn left at Wellington St W where the shiny **Ritz-Carlton** and the geometrical **Roy Thomson Hall** will compete left and right for your attention.

9 Take the path after the **Ritz-Carlton** to explore the art installations in **Simcoe Park**: the aluminum mountain by Anish Kapoor and the monument to workers.

On Front St W, near the life-size statue of Glen Gould on a bench, walk inside the **CBC** and across the building to admire the glass ceiling. Then exit on Wellington St W where you'll turn left to continue northbound on John St.

King Street W

On the **TIFF Bell Lightbox**'s 2nd floor, **Luma**'s inviting lounge offers a great view over King St, including the funky facade with half cows of the **Kit Kat Bar** across the street (polaroid **#10** on the map).

Walk east on King St W and explore the vast **David Pecaut Square**.

11 Make sure to look down at the foot of **Roy Thomson Hall** to view the surprisingly large pond you could not see from the street.

In the last few years, they've installed a patio over the pond to present free evening concerts while we have a bite and a drink. How civilized!

12 **St. Andrews Church** is next. You should enter to have a look at an example of elegant Romanesque architecture, with a unique round upper gallery and gorgeous stained glass windows.

Toronto Dominion

Two blocks further east, cross York St and turn right on York St. Look for the path between the first and second buildings, to access the **Toronto Dominion Centre** courtyard.

13 See the cows? They are the creation of Joe Fafard. Serene cows in the middle of the **Financial District**'s rat race. Hilarious, isn't it?

Commerce Court

14 Turn left on Wellington St W. Cross at Bay St and walk left. Around the first building, you will see the path to access the courtyard of **Commerce Court**. Now, we see elephants by a large fountain!

Exit into Melinda St, to Yonge St. Then... maybe a bite at **Sud Forno**?

NATHALIE'S **TIPS TO PLAN** THIS STROLL

For a shorter walk

I recommend this 3-km loop (45-min walk) encompassing a dog fountain, an eagle, cows and elephants. From King Subway Station, cross Yonge St and walk south, go left on Colborne St then right on Leader Lane. Follow #6 to #8. Walk across the vast **David Pecaut Square**, then follow #11 to #14.

About timing and logistics

• I usually end up parking in the **Green P** parking lot at the foot of Church St.
• You could combine this walk with a movie at the beautiful **TIFF Bell Lightbox** and King St W & John St. Check their calendar at **www.tiff.net**.

Romantic mood

• For an extra special date, I strongly recommend dinner at **Canoe**, on the 54th floor of the **Toronto Dominion Centre** (66 Wellington St W), see #13 for location. The view... over the **CN Tower**! The decor! The service! The food, so beautifully presented! Ideally, don't book dinner before 8:30 pm to avoid the less romantic (and noisier) business crowd with big expense accounts. Visit their gallery on **www.canoerestaurant.com**. Note that they are only open on weekdays, for lunch then from 5 pm to 10:30 pm.
• The **Roy Thomson Hall** normally offers a *Live on the Patio* series of evening concerts by the pond (see #11) in summertime, with food and bar service. Check **www.roythomsonhall.com** for updates.

Family fun

• Dog fountain, a giant eagle, cows and elephants. They are all adorable! But the dog fountain is a real winner! I've never seen it without laughing kids playing with the good dogs in **Berczy Park**. The water sprays spurting out of their mouth are irresistible. Maybe bring an extra set of clothes!
• I must say the **Old Spaghetti Factory** (54 The Esplanade, east of #7) is fun, with the dark vintage woodwork contrasting with the colourful ceiling busy with lamps, suspended carrousel horses and musical instruments. Kids love the dining section shaped like an old streetcar. Families appreciate the affordable prices and generous portions. Visit **www.oldspaghettifactory.net**.

A little extra in the area

• Check the mini-walks #3 and #4 on page 219 and #5 on page 220 in the last chapter **#torontourbangems**.

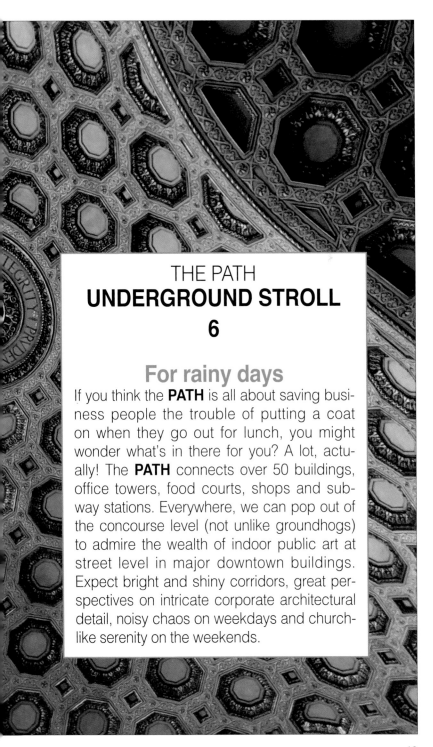

THE PATH
UNDERGROUND STROLL
6

For rainy days

If you think the **PATH** is all about saving business people the trouble of putting a coat on when they go out for lunch, you might wonder what's in there for you? A lot, actually! The **PATH** connects over 50 buildings, office towers, food courts, shops and subway stations. Everywhere, we can pop out of the concourse level (not unlike groundhogs) to admire the wealth of indoor public art at street level in major downtown buildings. Expect bright and shiny corridors, great perspectives on intricate corporate architectural detail, noisy chaos on weekdays and church-like serenity on the weekends.

STROLL
6

Toronto area
DOWNTOWN

Neighbourhood
Financial District

Full loop
4 km (6,155 steps)

Time estimate
1 hr

Mindset
When you are in the mood for a playful treasure hunt.

Subway & TTC
• This stroll starts at **Queen Subway Station** but the **PATH** is also connected to **Dundas**, **King**, **Union** and **St. Andrew Subway Stations**.

Best parking
• **City Hall**'s indoor parking (110 Queen W, $6/after 6 pm, $8/weekends) connects to the **Sheraton Hotel**.
• Go on **Best Parking app** (www.bestparking.com) and search **Saks Fifth Avenue, Toronto**.

Nathalie's TIPS
• See p. 55 for more tips to help you plan this walk.

First things first

1   **Saks Food Hall by Pusateri's**, in the lower level of **The Bay** (by **Queen Subway** exit) is the perfect starting point for this stroll. It opens at 7 am on weekdays, later on weekends. You can grab coffee and a bite (square doughnut, anyone?) at one of the counters. There are a few seats (and more tables further west on the floor).

Bay-Adelaide Centre

2   Past **Pusateri's**, turn left and take the escalators down to **Bay-Adelaide Centre**. Then walk through **Scotia Plaza** doors on your left and, all of a sudden, you'll be in a world of red granite.

In any building on the **PATH**, you'll see people in suits swarming the glossy corridors on weekdays. On weekends, when all the businesses and shops are closed, it's a totally different experience!

Scotia Plaza

3   Once you reach the elevators, walk through the corridor between elevators 23-39 and 55-65 and take the escalator up to admire the breathtaking *Waterfall* painting by Derek Besant in **Scotiabank**.

Double back down the escalator and around the **Second Cup** to **Commerce Court** (on the left fork).

Commerce Court

You'll enter the classy corridor with elaborate inlaid floor of **Commerce Court**. Go up the imposing staircase.

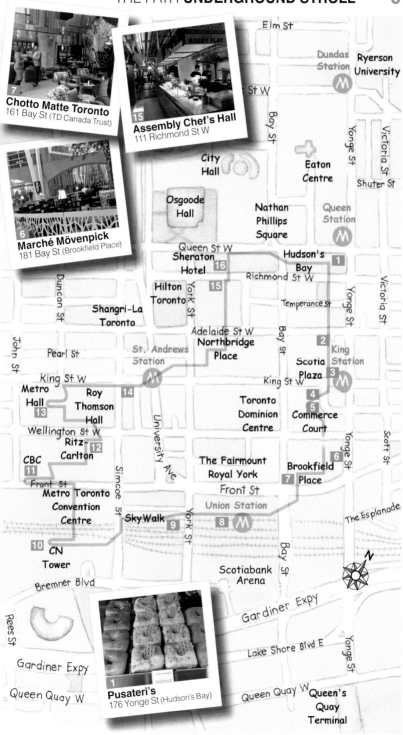

Chotto Matte Toronto
161 Bay St (TD Canada Trust)

Assembly Chef's Hall
111 Richmond St W

Marché Mövenpick
181 Bay St (Brookfield Place)

Pusateri's
176 Yonge St (Hudson's Bay)

Elm St

Dundas Station

Ryerson University

St W

Bay St

City Hall

Eaton Centre

Yonge St

Victoria St

Shuter St

Osgoode Hall

Nathan Phillips Square

Queen Station

Queen St W

Sheraton Hotel 16

Hudson's Bay 1

Richmond St W

Hilton Toronto 15

Shangri-La Toronto

Duncan St

York St

Temperance St

Victoria St

Adelaide St W
Northbridge Place

Bay St

John St

Pearl St

St. Andrews Station

King St W

Scotia Plaza 3

King Station

2

Metro Hall 13

Roy Thomson Hall

14

King St W

Toronto Dominion Centre

4
5
Commerce Court

Wellington St W

Ritz-Carlton 12

University Ave

Yonge St

Scott St

CBC 11

Front St

Metro Toronto Convention Centre

Simcoe St

The Fairmount Royal York

Brookfield Place 6

7

Front St

Union Station

SkyWalk 9

York St

8

The Esplanade

10 CN Tower

Scotiabank Arena

Bay St

Bremner Blvd

Rees St

Gardiner Expy

Lake Shore Blvd E

Yonge St

Gardiner Expy

Queen Quay W

Queen's Quay Terminal

Queen Quay W

4 On your left is **Commerce Court North**. Enter to see Toronto's most beautiful ceiling with a sea of undulating gold coffers, a magnificent piece of Art Deco from 1931. (Even if the building is closed, you will be able to admire it through the glass doors.)

On your right, you'll see elephants in the courtyard. If you can, peek outside, pass the revolving doors and enter the lobby of **Commerce Court West**. It now hosts an elegant **Dineen Coffee** (with a bar open until 8 pm on weekdays). Tempting... Maybe later?

5 Go down the escalators you'll see in the lobby. Turn right and walk past the inlaid compass rose on the floor.

Brookfield Place

Past **Rexall**, follow the signs to **BCE Place** and **Union Station** to **Brookfield Place**. It turns right at **Hockey Hall of Fame**'s exit (its entrance is one floor up).

6 Go up the escalators for a splendid view of the six-storey arches of the **Allen Lambert Galleria** juxtaposed with the heritage historic facade from the 1890's-era (which used to be on Wellington St). A perfect integration of old and new.

Further east, **Marché Mövenpick** used to be under the arches, but it closed in May 2020. Let's hope a cool restaurant will fill that void!

Tim Hortons by the **Hockey Hall of Fame** did a good job at playing the hockey theme.

Walk to the west side of **Brookfield Place**. Turn left, around the bay windows, and walk towards the splash of colour of the **Chotto Matte** mural. Go right through the white and beige corridor of the **TD Canada Trust Tower**.

7 **Chotto Matte** (at the end of the corridor, to your left) is a vibrant new restaurant offering Japanese-Peruvian cuisine. I recommend ending this stroll with drinks amidst its amazing urban jungle.

From the **TD Tower**'s corridor, take the escalators down. Turn left and follow sign to **Union Station**. There was still construction at the time of print but look for the **Royal Bank Plaza** sign on the right, then follow signs to **UP Express**.

Union Station

8 Past a series of large columns, turn left, push the doors and go up the stairs. Tada! You're in the Great Hall of **Union Station**.

9 Going westbound, look for signs to **Rogers Centre** and **CN Tower**. Past the **Travel Information** office, turn left, then right to reach the 500-metre long **SkyWalk**. You will pass the **UP Express** (leading to **Pearson Airport**). It includes a **Balzac's** coffee counter.

Take the escalators up and turn left. The glassed tunnel will take you to the **Metro Toronto Convention Centre**.

10 At the end, take the escalators on your left, down to the **South Building**, and the next two

escalators, to see the superb *Turtle Pond*, with frog and turtle inlays.

Climb back and turn left into the glassed tunnel to **North Building**. Go down the two flights of stairs and walk westbound. Take the exit by **Second Cup**, cross at the lights and look for **CBC**'s entrance by Glen Gould's statue.

11 Walk to the atrium to admire **CBC**'s spectacular glass ceiling and return near Front's entrance to take the escalators down.

12 Follow the sign for **RBC Centre** and **Ritz-Carlton**. You will pass long corridors with interesting pixelated photos. Turn right at the **Ritz Carlton** and follow the signs for **Roy Thomson Hall**.

13 At **Reitmans,** you will want to take **Metro Hall**'s entrance on your left to see great murals. Then, return to **Reitmans** and turn left.

14 Following the signs to **Roy Thomson Hall** and **St. Andrews Station**, you will climb up the new functioning piano staircase! Further will be the corridor along **Roy Thomson Hall**'s pond (empty in the winter).

Past **St. Andrews Station**, follow the long white corridor and signs to the **Sheraton Centre** (keeping to your left).

You will come across the **Assembly Chef's Hall**, a funky restaurant with multiple food counters (polaroid **#15** on map).

16 Past the red doors, climb up the hotel lobby's escalators to admire its unique rooftop waterfall. In the summer, you can walk around them!

NATHALIE'S **TIPS TO PLAN** THIS STROLL

For a shorter walk

This 2-km loop (30-min walk) includes most of my favourite gems on the **PATH**: the *Waterfall* painting, Toronto's best ceiling, **Brookfield Place**'s impressive arches and the **SkyWalk**. Off **King Subway Station**, follow #3 to #9 and return.

About timing and logistics

• Note that only the stores and restaurants with street access remain open on the weekends in the **PATH** during their regular hours. Exploring it on the weekend is a completely different experience.
• The access to **Hudson's Bay** is locked when the store is closed. Its hours are 10 am to 9 pm on weekdays, 9:30 am to 7 pm on Saturdays and 11 am to 6 pm on Sundays.

Romantic mood

• Eating or having cocktails at spectacular **Chotto Matte** (see ##7) would definitely be a special date! Visit **www.chotto-matte.com/toronto** to book.
• Once in **Metro Hall** (see #13) you can exit at King St W and go see a movie at the beautiful **TIFF Bell Lightbox**. Check their calendar at **www.tiff.net**.

Family fun

• You've got a young hockey lover? First visit the **Hockey Hall of Fame** and go for a little treat at nearby **Tim Hortons**, featuring a hockey theme (see description at #6). Visit **www.hhof.com** for details. Then go to Union Station (see #8), look for the signs to **Scotiabank Arena** (I can't be more precise because that section was still under construction at the time of print) and take the west exit to admire *Leafs Legends Row*, the life-size sculpture of eager legends at the bench.
• There is a great model of **CBC**'s building made out of Lego, located past the atrium (see #11), near the **CBC Kids Studio**. Such attention to detail, right down to the beehives on the rooftop. (Yes, I checked. CBC harvests honey!)
• They were sort of hidden behind a huge promo panel for television series *Schitt's Creek* the last time I visited **CBC**'s atrium so I'm not sure if they were about to put them away, but for a few years now they've installed two fantastic giant Muskoka chairs entirely made out of sports equipment, one for winter sports and the other for summer sports, each called a *Throne of Games*. Hopefully, they are still there.
• Don't miss the chance for your kids to try the piano staircase (see #14)!

A little extra in the area

• Check the mini-walks #4 on page 219 and #7 on page 221 in the last chapter **#torontourbangems**.

QUEENS QUAY
HARBOURFRONT STROLL
7

Harbourfront and beyond

There's so much going on at **Harbourfront Centre** that it's easy to moor there and forget about setting sail further west to admire what lies ahead: the sculptural **Simcoe WaveDeck** (which also serves as a stylish boardwalk), the yellow umbrellas of **HTO Park**, the **Toronto Music Garden**, the tall totem of **Little Norway Park** and the impressive installation in remote **Ireland Park** facing the **CN Tower** across the channel (a tribute to the 38,000 Irish immigrants who arrived here in 1847 to escape the Great Potato Famine). All of them by the water!

STROLL
7

Toronto area
DOWNTOWN

Neighbourhood
**Bathurst Quay
+ Harbourfront**

Full loop
3.8 km (5,845 steps)

Time estimate
1 hr

Mindset
When you want to feel like one of the millions of tourists marveling at Toronto's unique mix of modernity, culture and nature.

Subway & TTC
• At **Union Subway Station**, catch **509** Harbourfront or **510** Spadina streetcars, on the underground platform, to Queens Quay Ferry Docks Terminal.

Best parking
• Go on **Best Parking app** (www.bestparking.com) and search **Harbourfront Centre**.

Nathalie's TIPS
• See p. 63 for more tips to help you plan this walk.

First things first

1 An excellent meeting point for this walk is the **Boxcar Social** overlooking the **Natrel Pond** (the former location of Lakeside Eats), for great coffee, cool vibes and tasty bites.

2 Save **Harbourfront's** artistic fun for later, and walk around the pond to the waterfront lined with touring boats, with **Toronto's Islands** in the background. Go right and cross over the white pedestrian bridge.

3 To your left is the very popular **Amsterdam Brewhouse** with multiple patios on two floors. If you can't get an outdoor seat (with the seagulls), you will find that the decor inside the vast restaurant has character.

The WaveDecks

4 Walking towards Queens Quay, you can't miss the sculptured **Simcoe WaveDeck**. It is part of a series of three **WaveDecks**, with two more to be seen further at Rees St and Spadina Ave.

As you walk westbound on Queens Quay, make sure you are not run over by a bike! Many cyclists don't realize how confusing it is for tourists and Torontonians not familiar with the area to make the distinction between the bike path and the pedestrian section. Now you know!

HTO Park

5 You can't swim at this urban beach, but it offers the fun combo of yellow umbrellas in the sand by the lake on one side, and the **CN Tower** on the other.

Off the map ←

13 · 14
10 · 12 · 11
Eireann Quay

N

9 · Ireland
8 · Park · 7

Bathurst St

Queens Quay W

Lake Shore Blvd W

Gardiner Expy

6

Toronto
Music Garden

Lower Spadina Ave

Lake Shore Blvd W

Queens Quay W

Bremner Blvd

5
HTO
Park

Rees St

Gardiner Expy

3

4

2 · 1
Harbourfront
Centre

Simcoe St

Lower

The Power
Plant

York St

Boxcar Social
235 Queens Quay W

Amsterdam BrewHouse
245 Queens Quay W

Aroma
4 Eireann Quay

Toronto Music Garden

6 Simply gorgeous! It is the combined vision of a cellist and a landscape designer with Bach in mind.

Signs in the garden will explain to you that Yo-Yo Ma and Julie Moir Messervy were inspired by Bach's *Cello Suite No.1 in G Major, BWV 1007*. To learn more about the musical theme associated with dance movements, you can rent a $6 audio wand for a 70-minute self-guided tour, at **Marina Quay West**, near the garden's western entrance.

Ireland Park

Two hidden gems await by the **Waterfront Neighbourhood Centre**.

7 Following the paved path towards the silos by the lake, you will notice bronze letters and fossil-like sculptures embedded into the pavement.

The inspiration for this art installation by Sarah Nind is a footnote from 1832 by Toronto's first surveyor, Joseph Bouchette. Start reading it from north to south and then back.

8 Walk around the silos to discover the life-size statues of emaciated Irish people overlooking downtown Toronto in **Ireland Park**. This is the impressive monument to over 38,000 Irish immigrants who reached Toronto by boat in 1847.

Rowan Gillespie, who had previously sculpted *Departure* (a similar series set on the waterfront of Dublin) was asked to create a group of sculptures depicting their arrival here.

9 He completed it with a boat-like limestone structure. Further west is Toronto's downtown airport.

Billy Bishop Airport

The **Billy Bishop Toronto City Airport** includes **Porter Airlines** and **Air Canada** check-in counters on the mainland, as well as an **Aroma** take-out counter (polaroid **#10** on the map). The actual airport is located on **Toronto Islands**.

11 You can still catch the shortest ferry ride ever across the canal (it's free) but a very welcome pedestrian tunnel was added in 2015. Take the elevator down to the 260-metre tunnel with moving walkways.

12 Then 153 steps in one of Canada's longest escalator systems leads you to the airport, where you'll see a plane replica and historical artifacts paying tribute to Billy Bishop, the war hero.

Artsy finish

13 Back to the mainland, turn around the airport to access **Little Norway Park**. You'll notice an impressive lion in the playground!

14 A superb totem sits closer to Queens Quay. Quite the gem!

There's more art to be enjoyed back to **Harbourfront Centre**: artists in action in their studios inside the centre, great free exhibitions at **The Power Plant**, near the pond, and gorgeous brass fish embedded in the sidewalk at the southwest corner of York St and Queens Quay W.

NATHALIE'S **TIPS TO PLAN** THIS STROLL

For a shorter walk
I suggest a 2.2-km loop (35-min walk), which includes the **Toronto Music Garden** and **Ireland Park**. Simply follow #6 to #14.

About timing and logistics
• It truly is important to be vigilant not to wander onto the bike path when you walk along Queens Quay W! At peak times, there can be over 500 cyclists flashing by and the distinction between bike lane and pedestrian path is very subtle.

Romantic mood
• If you go towards the canal past the playground (see #13) and turn right to reach the end of the pier, you will find a great spot to watch sunsets.
• You don't need to be a guest at the **Radisson Admiral Hotel** to have a cocktail at its poolside bar on the fifth floor while admiring the lake, but you'll need to be one to use the pool. At the time of print, they were announcing that the hotel would be renamed **Radisson Blu Toronto Downtown**. See **www.radissonhotels.com** for updates.
• There's always something interesting at **The Power Plant**, featuring pay-what-you-can contemporary art exhibitions, where the installations have enough room to breathe, and visitors ample space to move. It never was too crowded on the several occasions I've visited. Visit **www.thepowerplant.org** for updates.

Family fun
• In summertime, you can rent paddle boats at **Natrel Pond** (see #2).
• I think no kids will resist the fun of riding the moving walkways and the long escalators of the pedestrian tunnel linking the mainland to the airport (see #11). It's free! And it's right next to the playground with the giant lion (see #13).
• Also free, the smallest ferry ride ever (150 metres) crossing the canal to reach the airport.

A little extra in the area
• If you cross Queens Quay W at #7 and go north on Dan Leckie Way, you will be only 200 metres away from #7 of the *PORTLAND STREET Utterly Urban Stroll* (see page 69).
• You could continue your walk east of **Harbourfront Centre** with the *East Bayfront WATERFRONT Stroll* (see page 32).

PORTLAND STREET
UTTERLY URBAN STROLL
8

Go big or stay home!

Have you noticed all the large pieces of public art in unexpected places? It's due to the special *Percent for Public Art Program* established by the City of Toronto in 2010, which requires that Toronto developers allocate 1% of the gross cost of their development to public art. My favourite is the huge bobbers in **Canoe Landing Park** off Fort York Blvd, but there's enough public art in the area to make this walk amidst over-towering condos an intriguing one worth the detour. King & Portland intersection is more vibrant than ever with all the restaurants, bars and cafés supported by the influx of condo dwellers. The **Stackt Market**, **The Bentway** and **Graffiti Alley** bring their colourful vibe to the area.

STROLL
8

Toronto area
DOWNTOWN

Neighbourhood
Fashion District
+ Entertainment
District

Full loop
5.1 km (7,845 steps)

Time estimate
1 hr 20 min

Mindset
When you are in a
"Go big or go home!"
state of mind and
want to feel utterly
urban.

Subway & TTC
• Streetcars **501**, **511**.

Best parking
• Go on **Best Park-
ing app** (www.best-
parking.com) and
search **Graffiti Alley,
Toronto**.

Nathalie's TIPS
• See p. 71 for more
tips to help you plan
this walk.

First things first

1 Now that I have had a
taste of their pink Eggs
Benedict and the joy of dig-
ging into an avocado rose,
I always use this walk as an
excuse to go to **Early Bird
Coffee & Kitchen**. Their
seating arrangement is not
the most comfortable but
they definitely serve some of
the prettiest dishes in town!

I suggest you save
the **Graffiti Alley** for the
end but if you absolutely
can't resist, it is the first
lane to your left as you walk
southbound on Portland St.

2 Further down awaits
Jimmy's Coffee,
across the street from...
another **Jimmy's Coffee**!
The newest, on the west
side of Portland St, occupies
two floors. Did you know
that all the **Jimmy's** feature
murals of famous Jimmys?

There's an aura of
coolness around Portland
St, despite all the new
modern condos, that I find
very appealing. The exotic
**Chubby's Jamaican Kitch-
en** in the old house near
Jimmy's sets the tone.

Portland & King

On King St W, the likes of
über cool sausage place
WVRST and the Italian
bakery **Forno Cultura** in an
industrial semi-basement
mingle with trendy rooftop
Lavelle, striking Italian restaurant **Oretta** and stylish
Asian fusion **Lee**.

3 Sure values still hang
around Wellington St
W, further south, pass the
corridor of mid-size con-
dos: **Bar Wellington**, a
classic pub, **Marben**, with
its gorgeous wooden ceiling,

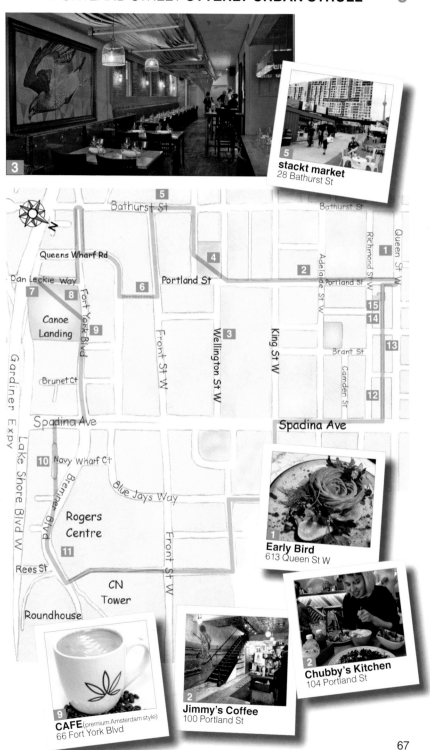

stackt market
28 Bathurst St

Early Bird
613 Queen St W

Chubby's Kitchen
104 Portland St

Jimmy's Coffee
100 Portland St

CAFE (premium Amsterdam style)
66 Fort York Blvd

and classy French bistro **Le Sélect**. All the above would be interesting options after the stroll, depending on the time of the day.

4 At Portland & Wellington, you will cross the **Victoria Memorial Square**, at the location of Toronto's oldest cemetery. (A few unbroken tombstones were dug up.)

Turn west on Niagara St. Peak inside the Scandinavian-inspired **Thor Espresso Bar** and cross Bathurst St to reach the **stackt market**.

5 **Stackt** is a new market concept making good use of shipping containers, with plenty of cool outdoor public space to chill, plus a brewery. In the shops-in-a-container there are retailers as well as providers of donuts, bubble tea, coffee, noodles, etc.

Front Street East

6 Walk eastbound on Front St W and use the impressive pedestrian bridge to cross over the train tracks. *Puente de Luz* (bridge of light) is the amazing design by Chilean Francisco Gazitua. (You will recognize his touch in many other artworks along the stroll. Even the lampposts match the concept.)

Follow Queens Wharf Rd to your right. The modern architecture of the **Library District Condos** to your right on Fort York Blvd is beautiful.

If you walked past Bathurst, you'd reach the historic **Fort York** and **The Bentway**, the exciting new public space under the

Gardiner Expy pillars (featuring a rink in winter time).

Canoe Landing

Turn left on Fort York Blvd, then right onto Dan Leckie Way. You are now surrounded by the high-rises of **City Place**. As you go down, you will notice lovely metal cut outs on your right.

7 Cross over towards the park and walk up the dirt path. (If slippery after a rain or a bit steep for you, walk up the sidewalk to a staircase taking you to **Canoe Landing Park**.)

Douglas Coupland, the artist/author who coined the expression "generation x", is responsible for the giant red canoe in the southwest corner of the park. It is large enough for drivers to notice from the Gardiner Expy and you can hop in.

8 I am in awe of the fishing bobbers/splash pad by the same artist, closer to Fort York Blvd. They are so whimsical, in this serious surrounding.

The paved path running around the field is the **Terry Fox Miracle Mile**, a circuit marked by more intriguing art by Coupland.

Across the street is the slick **CAFE** serving excellent coffee and treats, and a 2nd floor filled with goodies "premium Amsterdam style"... (see #9 on map)!

Further east, you will see the new modern **Canoe Landing Community Recreation Centre** (including two elementary schools and a daycare). Cross Spadina Ave at the light and go south on the other side.

Bremner Boulevard

At the top of the stairs to your left, turn around to admire the artwork across Spadina Ave then walk to Mariner Terrace to see its big sister!

10 *Barca Volante*, from the artist who did the pedestrian bridge, is an immense steel sculpture gracefully standing over a reflecting pool, which adds airy lightness to the piece.

11 Go east to a short cut leading to Bremner Blvd and walk around **Rogers Centre**. Notice the bronze fish swimming up a river in the beautiful *Salmon Run* fountain by Susan Schelle. Further, **Ripley's Aquarium** sits at the foot of the **CN Tower**.

Closer to Front St E, look up **Rogers Centre** to enjoy the mischievous giants leaning over the balcony.

Go northbound on John St, turn left at Wellington St W then right into Blue Jays Way. That street has changed tremendously, with the likes of designer **Bisha Hotel Toronto** (80 Blue Jays Way) with the beachhouse like breezy rooftop **Kost** on the 44th floor, open daily from 7am!

The Graffiti Alley

12 Turn left at King St W and cross at Spadina Ave, then walk northbound, and turn left into the **Graffiti Alley** past Richmond St W. It starts with edgier graffiti but gets intricate as you proceed towards Portland St (see **#13** and **#14** on map).

15 The hidden **Alex Wilson Community Garden** is a beautiful surprise., closer to Portland St.

NATHALIE'S **TIPS TO PLAN** THIS STROLL

For a shorter walk

For a 3-km (45-min walk) version of the full loop, follow #1 to #4 but don't go west on Niagara St. Instead, walk through the opening into the townhouse complex on the south side of **Victoria Memorial Square**. An interesting setting, right? Then walk through the municipal parking lot onto Front St. Follow #6 but don't go right on Queens Wharf Rd, turn left and take the first street to your right to reach **Canoe Landing Park**. See #7 and #8 then walk eastbound on Fort York Blvd to Spadina Rd, and turn left. Walk north to the Graffiti Alley (see #12 to #15 on the map).

About timing and logistics

• The **Green P** at Portland & Front offers a $5 flat rate after 6 pm.

Romantic mood

• All the public art along this stroll is nicely lit at night!

• Go chill at the **Stackt Market** (see #5). Check their website **www.stackt market.com** to find out about their current events and see their list of merchants.

• In wintertime, consider **The Bentway Skate Trail**, on Fort York Blvd west of Bathurst (they rent skates). At other times, look them up to see if one of their cool events is going on. See **www.thebentway.ca** for updates.

• On the second Friday of every month in **Ripley's Aquarium** (at the foot of the CN Tower), there is live jazz and they install cash bars throughout the aquarium. To buy a ticket, go to **www.ripleyaquariums.com/canada**.

• The dark **BarChef** at 472 Queen St W is your chance to try a theatrical cocktail wrapped in the thick fog of dry ice! See **www.barchef.com**.

Family fun

• **Fort York National Historic Site** is located at 250 Fort York Blvd. The **Visitors Centre** is gorgeous. You can see a fantastic 15-min long movie on three screens explaining the history of the area. Then you get to walk through a multimedia installation simulating a trench before exiting to explore the historic buildings of the fort. See **www.fortyork. ca** for details.

• The giant fishing bobbers installation in **Canoe Landing Park** (see #8) is also a refreshing splash pad in summertime.

• The **Graffiti Alley** is filled with animals to spot! Kids especially dig Uber 5000's large mural depicting Canadian landmarks on the west wall of the hugely popular fish mural, also by this artist (see #13).

A little extra in the area

• Check the mini-walk #8 on page 221 and #14 on page 224 in the last chapter **#torontourbangems**.

KENSINGTON/CHINATOWN
TRULY ECLECTIC STROLL
9

Colourful and funky mix

OK, this is not exactly a walk to burn off calories. You'll want to stop every ten metres to explore it all. There truly is a special vibe to both high-density neighbourhoods offering a unique combo of residential and commercial. **Kensington Market**, where old bargain stores mingle with slick urban boutiques and vintage shops sit next to bulk ethnic markets, is funkier and more laidback. Nearby **Chinatown** means business. Its exotic shops and restaurants along Spadina and Dundas are bustling with busy people, all the way to the **AGO**. In both neighbourhoods, carnivores and vegetarians mix peacefully and colourful murals and graffiti add to the eclectic appeal.

STROLL
9

Toronto area
DOWNTOWN

Neighbourhood
Kensington Market
+ Chinatown
+ Grange Park

Full loop
4.4 km (6,155 steps)

Time estimate
1 hr 05 min

Mindset
When you want to take a walk on the wild side... of Toronto.

Subway & TTC
• Get off at **Osgoode Station** and do a 4-min walk westbound.
• Streetcar **501**.

Best parking
• Go on **Best Parking app** (www.bestpark-ing.com) and search **Kensington Market**.

Nathalie's TIPS
• See p. 79 for more tips to help you plan this walk.

First things first

1 Popular **HotBlack Coffee** is a 2-min walk from **Osgoode Subway Station**. I was seduced by its small backyard patio and post-industrial vibe.

2 Not many know that **The Rex Jazz & Blues Bar** across the street is a hotel and that, as such, they open early and have sturdy and affordable breakfast options on their menu.

3 While you're here, you might want to check the intriguing half house at 54 1/2 St. Patrick St. Apparently, the owner never wanted to sell to the developer!

Around the AGO

From McCaul St (or St. Patrick St) find Renfrew Pl (the small street just north of Queen St W) and walk westbound to John St. Then turn right at **Umbra Store** (their flagship boutique displaying the whole Umbra collection).

Walk into the **Grange Park Promenade** to reach the park. Along the way, you'll see 14 quotations inscribed in paving stones.

4 **Grange Park** is truly impressive! To your left, Henry Moore's *Two Large Forms* chill under the trees. Facing you, the 1817 Georgian manor (which lends its name to the park) looks like it melted into the **AGO** four-storey blue titanium wall.

5 To your right, a new creative playground blends beautifully with the modern structure of the **OCAD**. Walk under its tall pillars to McCaul St.

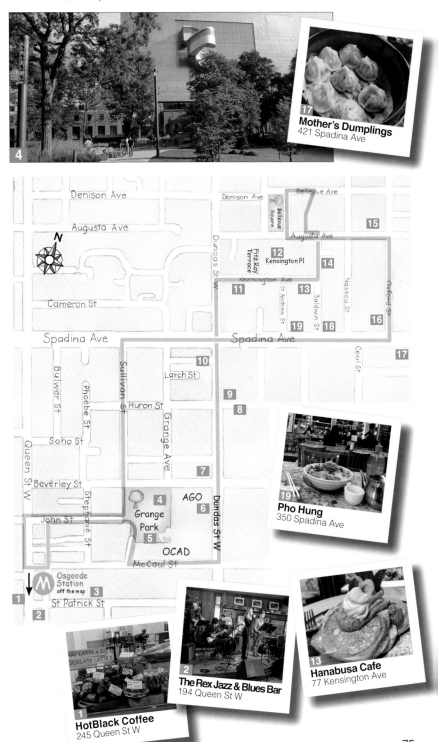

17
Mother's Dumplings
421 Spadina Ave

4

Denison Ave

Augusta Ave

Bellevue Ave

Denison Ave

Bellevue Square

Augusta Ave

15

N

Dundas St

Fitz Ray Terrace

12 Kensington Pl

14

Cameron St

Kensington Ave

11

13

St Andrew St

Baldwin St

Nassau St

Oxford St

Spadina Ave

Spadina Ave

19

18

16

Cecil St

17

10

Larch St

Bulwer St

Phoebe St

Sullivan St

Huron St

Grange Ave

9

8

Soho St

7

19
Pho Hung
350 Spadina Ave

Beverley St

AGO

4

6

Stephanie St

Grange Park

Dundas St W

John St

5

OCAD

McCaul St

Osgoode Station
off the map **3**

1

2

St Patrick St

1
HotBlack Coffee
245 Queen St W

2
The Rex Jazz & Blues Bar
194 Queen St W

13
Hanabusa Cafe
77 Kensington Ave

Walk around the very well stocked **Above Ground Art Supplies** into Dundas St W. Before taking your left, turn around to face south and take in the panorama of the **OCAD** with the **CN Tower** in the background.

6 The museum's architecture on Dundas St W is spectacular, with the glass structure rising 70 feet above street level, like a giant Noah's ark. It marks the beginning of **Chinatown**.

Dundas St West

7 **Lucky Moose Food Mart** features a survivor from the *Moose in the City* project of 2000 when 326 such life-sized moose invaded the town. Its busy facade is typical of **Chinatown**.

The next two blocks are jam-packed with small shops of all sorts well attended by clients of Asian descent. It's like travelling, without paying for a plane ticket!

8 The **Chinatown BIA** (Business Improvement Area) has commissioned many themed murals to be admired in the lanes off Dundas St W.

9 The latest public art produced for the **BIA**, located on Huron St, north of Dundas St W, represents the Chinese Zodiac signs.

10 Around the corner, **Ten Ren's Tea** shop carries a vast selection of teas and original tea pots.

Walk westbound on Dundas St W, beyond Spadina Ave, to explore a different kind of effervescence.

Kensington Avenue

Turn right onto Kensington Ave. It is my favourite part of **Kensington Market** because most of this section is chock-full of funky vintage clothing stores. (If you were a teen in the 70's, chances are you'll recognize most of the stuff in these shops...)

11 You don't need to be a fan of the bohemian style to be charmed by the candy coloured facades on the street and the whimsical clothes inside the likes of: **Exile**, **Flashback**, **Courage My Love** or **Dancing Days**, to name a few.

12 Explore Fitz Roy Terrace and Kensington Pl, the two dead-end streets you will find on the west side of Kensington Ave, to see the funkiest residential nooks in Toronto.

Along the way, I like slick **FIKA Cafe** (28 Kensington Ave) for the beautiful lattes and snacks, and their wall plastered with book pages, laidback **Moonbean Coffee** (30 St. Andrews St) the long and narrow café with large backyard, and the decadent Japanese soufflé pancakes at **Hanabusa Café** (polaroid **#13** on map).

14 Turn left at Baldwin St, the heart of the market for bakeries, cheese store, nut importers, fruit and vegetable stalls, bargain stores, and **Jimmy's Coffee** (191 Baldwin St) with its industrial lounge and a fantastic back patio.

Augusta Avenue

Turn left at Augusta Ave and take the little passage right

after **King's Café** (192 Augusta Ave). Walk through the large parking lot then turn left on Bellevue Ave to reach the cute **Bellevue Square Park**. Continue northbound to explore Augusta Ave.

15 I love to browse in **Blue Banana Market,** a marketplace with the feel of a souk. Across the street is **Bungalow** (273 Augusta Ave), a trendy lifestyle store including retro vintage clothing and furniture. Further north, **Fresh Collective** (274 Augusta Ave) curates a cool selection of local designers.

16 Turn east on Oxford St to reach Spadina Ave. See the picture ready dragon mural on your right?

Spadina Avenue

Across Spadina Ave, you'll find **Mother's Dumplings**, a pretty and affordable restaurant where you can watch staff preparing the dumplings (polaroid **#17** on map).

Walking southbound on Spadina Ave, you can see cooks at work through the restaurants' windows, exotic offerings on the outdoor stalls, and red dragons perched on tall poles.

18 My favourite place to peruse for merchandise I don't see anywhere else is **B & J Trading** but there are many other shops to discover.

19 **Pho Hung**, near the cat column, is a bright place serving generous portions of good Vietnamese dishes.

Continue southbound on Spadina Ave and turn left on Sullivan St. back to **Grange Park**.

NATHALIE'S **TIPS TO PLAN** THIS STROLL

For a shorter walk

You can easily break this stroll into two shorter walks each exploring one neighbourhood. For the 2.8-km loop (45-min walk) covering **Chinatown** and the **AGO**, follow #1 to #10, then cross at Spadina Ave and turn right. Cross on the east side of Spadina Ave at St. Andrews St. Then follow #19 back to **Grange Park**. For the 1.75-km loop (30-min walk) exploring **Kensington Market**, follow #11 to #16, and go southbound back to Dundas St W.

About timing and logistics

• In summertime from 12 noon to 7 pm, the **Kensington Market** is at its liveliest during their **Pedestrian Sundays**. Visit **www.kensington-market.ca** for updates.

• **Kensington Market** is also the place holding the **Winter Solstice Festival** every December 21. Organized by **Red Pepper Spectacle Arts**, it involves a cool lantern march through the market's streets, music and big bonfire. Visit **www.redpepperspectacle.com** for details.

• Interesting fact: Toronto's first **Chinatown** was exprpriated in the late 1950s to build **Nathan Phillips Square** and the **New City Hall**. The downtown Chinatown we know (one of the largest in North America) was formerly a Jewish district, which explains the historical value of **Gwartzman's Art Supplies** (448 Spadina Ave), established in 1945 in the same building (with the 3rd generation of Gwartzmans still running the business)!

Romantic mood

• How about the easy to miss **Poetry Jazz Café** (224 Augusta Ave) with the "poetry" word in neon on a black facade? The small cocktail bar with live new jazz, neo soul, poetry and spoken word. See **www.poetryjazzcafe.com** for details.

• **AGO** offers free admission every Wednesday from 6-9 pm. Free tickets are issued to visitors in person, starting at 6 pm. Save your money for a nice meal!

Family fun

• The **Grange Park** features one of Toronto's best playgrounds! The art theme is truly original. Can your kids recognize a spilled paint can, crumpled paper, a charcoal pencil tower and a squished paint tube climbable sculpture?

• The **AGO Family Sundays** are really fun. See **www.ago.ca/family-sundays** for details. Remember that admission is free for 25 years and under.

A little extra in the area

• Check the mini-walk #16 on page 225 in the last chapter **#torontourbangems**.

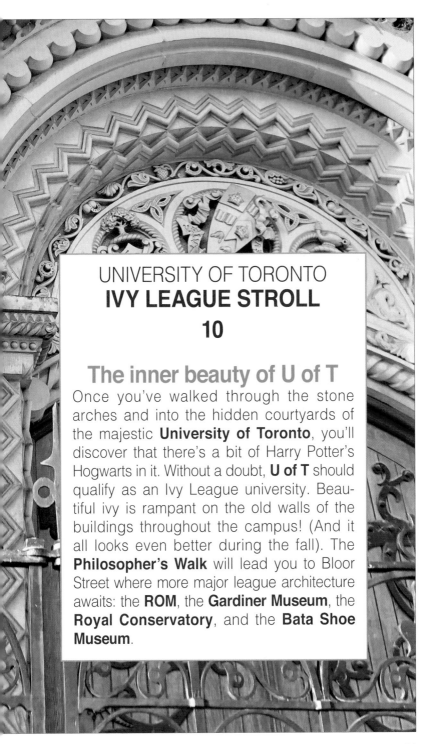

UNIVERSITY OF TORONTO
IVY LEAGUE STROLL
10

The inner beauty of U of T

Once you've walked through the stone arches and into the hidden courtyards of the majestic **University of Toronto**, you'll discover that there's a bit of Harry Potter's Hogwarts in it. Without a doubt, **U of T** should qualify as an Ivy League university. Beautiful ivy is rampant on the old walls of the buildings throughout the campus! (And it all looks even better during the fall). The **Philosopher's Walk** will lead you to Bloor Street where more major league architecture awaits: the **ROM**, the **Gardiner Museum**, the **Royal Conservatory**, and the **Bata Shoe Museum**.

STROLL 10

Toronto area
DOWNTOWN

Neighbourhood
University
+ Bay Street Corridor

Full loop
4.4 km (6,770 steps)

Time estimate
1 hr 05 min

Mindset
When you want to put yourself in the shoes of Harry Potter entering Hogwarts.

Subway & TTC
• Exit at **St. George Subway Station** (if you don't want to stop for coffee first, you can exit at **Museum Subway Station** and start the loop at #16, going backwards.

Best parking
• Go on **Best Parking app** (www.bestpark-ing.com) and search **Bata Shoe Museum.**

Nathalie's TIPS
• See p. 87 for more tips to help you plan this walk.

First things first

1 The 2-min walk from **St. George Subway Station** to my favourite meeting point for this walk includes a chance to admire the gorgeous display of the **Bata Shoe Museum** on the way.

2 **L'Espresso Bar Mercurio** looks elegant and breezy, with the long drapes and columns, and a lovely garden patio. Many **U of T** professors eat here so the café opens at 7:30 am on weekdays and 9 am on the weekends.

3 Enter the **Royal Conservatory** (273 Bloor St W) and turn left to marvel at its stunning architecture, blending the old with the new. The **b espresso bar** is located in the atrium.

4 Walk straight to exit into the **Philosopher's Walk**. (If arriving from Bloor St W, you will pass through majestic black iron gates.)

Trinity College

You can access **Trinity College** off this path but for a more dramatic effect, I suggest you continue to Hoskin Ave and turn right to enter the imposing building from its main entrance.

5 Walk across the building to exit into the magnificent courtyard with a unique patterned path. This concept of open air space surrounded by buildings on all sides is called a quadrangle.

6 On your way back to the front door, take the corridor on your right to discover another hidden

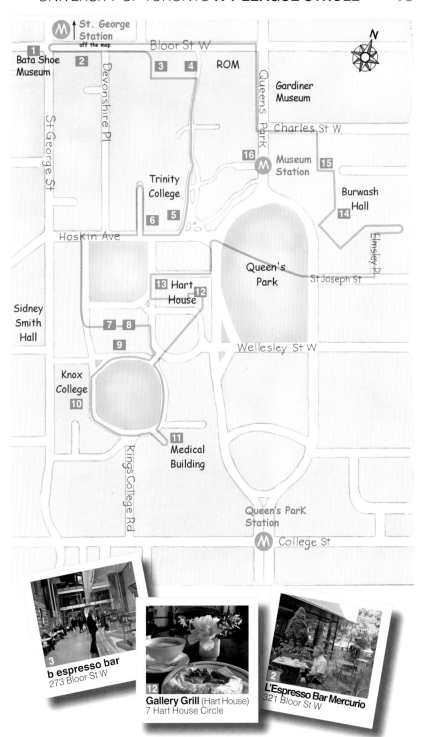

St. George Station
off the map

Bata Shoe Museum

Bloor St W

Devonshire Pl

ROM

Queens Park

Gardiner Museum

Charles St W

St George St

Museum Station

Burwash Hall

Trinity College

Hoskin Ave

Queen's Park

St Joseph St

Elmsley Pl

Sidney Smith Hall

Hart House

Knox College

Wellesley St W

Kings College Rd

Medical Building

Queen's Park Station

College St

b espresso bar
273 Bloor St W

Gallery Grill (Hart House)
7 Hart House Circle

L'Espresso Bar Mercurio
321 Bloor St W

treasure: the elegant **Trinity College Chapel**. This gem of unpretentious beauty is the last design of the English architect who created the Liverpool Cathedral and... British red phone booths!

Make sure you don't miss the carved details down the arches all around, with animal theme on one side and sports focus on the other. They are hilarious!

King's College Circle

Cross the street and walk eastbound on Hoskin Ave. Then take the cobbled path on your left along the field.

7 You will reach a space with multiple paths. Behind the doors of **St. George Campus** on your left is hidden another quadrangle and a series of beautiful wooden arches. Enter through the left door to find your way to the courtyard.

8 Walk straight to the next door and exit. And voilà! The historic arches are on your right. Go through the colonnades, past the **Art Museum**. Enter the building, turn right and left to exit into Hart House Circle.

9 Go right on King's College Circle to admire **St. George**'s spectacular main entrance.

10 **Knox College** is equally breathtaking. You must enter to see the courtyard through the cloister's gothic windows (great architectural choice since **Knox** grants theology degrees).

11 Contrast all this classical architecture with the modern take of the

Medical Sciences Building at 1 King's College Circle. (Walk around the building to the left of the entrance for interesting modern art.)

All around the circle, it gets truly spectacular during the fall, when the ivy covering the heritage buildings changes colour.

Continue north on the circle, and walk through the park on your right to get to **Hart House**. Up the stairs, admire a lovely deer cutout on your right before entering into the building.

12 Take the stairs in the corridor to your left and you will find the **Gallery Grill** on your right. Lunch is expensive but you can go early to have a coffee and a breakfast snack as the place opens daily from 8 am to 2 pm on weekdays and from 11 am to 2 pm on Saturdays.

13 Turn right on Tower Rd and take the time to carefully observe the bronze sculpture of a face on your right. Slowly walk around to see the full face morph into a profile. How clever is that!

Past the sculpture, go around the building and turn right into the lane to reach the street, then right again to the corner of Hoskin Ave and Queen's Park Crescent W to cross over to **Queen's Park**.

Elmsley Place

Walk through **Queen's Park** to get to St. Joseph St and turn left on Elmsley Place. Here, it feels more like a village than a campus, especially if you turn right past the houses to reach the church.

At the church, make a sharp left into the narrow path. It leads to a large courtyard. Walk through the arch behind the tall modern sculpture, then right again, around the **Pontifical Institute**.

Burwash Hall

14 My favourite thing on the campus east of Queen's Park Crescent is being greeted by the cheerful sound of water falling into the pond by **Burwash Hall**.

To reach the series of Neo-Gothic student housing covered in ivy, you'll need to cross the path by the statue of the two ladies and pass between two buildings.

15 Further, to your left, you can't miss the majestic **Victoria University**. Around it, you'll notice the intriguing statue of a crucified woman by **Emmanuel College**.

16 Keep walking towards Charles St, and take the underpass at Queen's Quay Crescent W to reach the **ROM** on the other side. It is also where you can access the unique **Museum Subway Station**.

NATHALIE'S **TIPS TO PLAN** THIS STROLL

For a shorter walk

This 2.7-km loop (40-min walk) includes two of the main gems on the campus: **Trinity College**'s quadrangle and **Knox College**'s spectacular architecture. Follow #1 to #6 then keep going until you reach King's College Circle and turn right. Walk to **Knox College** (see #10) and explore it inside (you can also visit their gorgeous library) and out (you can visit the courtyard). Continue around King's College Circle, and walk under the **Soldiers' Tower** (with a clock) and follow #13 (don't miss the amazing sculpture). Then don't cross to **Queen's Park**, keep going to reach **Museum Subway Station**.

About timing and logistics

• Parking on the campus is very expensive for visitors. You'll be better off finding municipal parking around Bloor St W. (I have had luck with paid street parking on St. George St, north of Lowther Ave.)

Romantic mood

• Grab Italian sandwiches and pastries at **L'Espresso Bar Mercurio** (see #2) and head to a lovely British-looking nook on the campus. It is surprisingly easy to find beautiful quiet spots, despite the fact that there are over 60,000 students at U of T. My favourite romantic spots are: the unique quadrangle of **Trinity College** (see #5), the inner courtyard of **St. George Campus** (see #8) right by the Art Museum (see details on **www.artmuseum.utoronto.ca**), and the bucolic pond by **Burwash Hall** (see #14).

• Book a fancy lunch at the **Gallery Grill** (see #11). Try to get a table by the windows overlooking the **Great Hall**.

• The **Koerner Hall** is Toronto's most beautiful venue, with impeccable acoustics and a breathtaking wooden ceiling. Check its programming on **www.rcmusic.com/performance** for your next musical date night, complete with a stroll on the **Philosopher's Walk** (see #3 and #4).

• Explore the **ROM** with a drink in hand during their **ROM After Dark** events, once a month on Friday night from 7 pm to 11:30 pm ($24/for 19+ students, $30/non-students, includes one complimentary drink). See **www.rom.on.ca/en/whats-on/rom-after-dark** for details.

Family fun

• The spots on the campus with the strongest Harry Potter vibe are the inner courtyard of **St. George Campus** (see #8), the inside of **Knox College** (see #10), and the **Great Hall** within **Hart House** (located at #12).
• Check the exciting **Museum Subway Station** (see #16)!

A little extra in the area

• Check the mini-walk #20 on page 227 in the last chapter **#torontourbangems**.

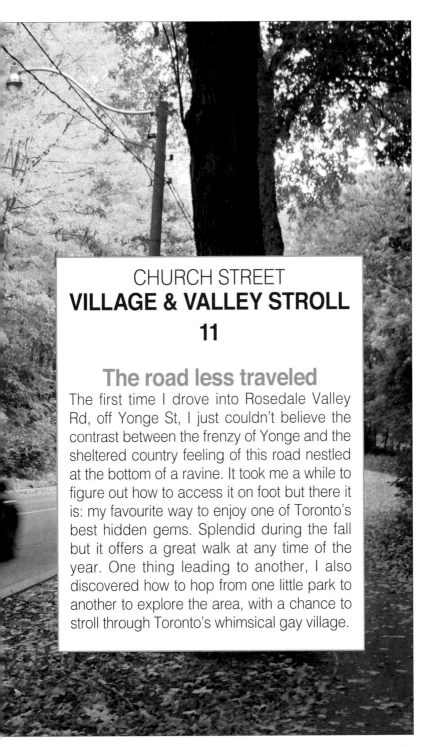

CHURCH STREET
VILLAGE & VALLEY STROLL
11

The road less traveled

The first time I drove into Rosedale Valley Rd, off Yonge St, I just couldn't believe the contrast between the frenzy of Yonge and the sheltered country feeling of this road nestled at the bottom of a ravine. It took me a while to figure out how to access it on foot but there it is: my favourite way to enjoy one of Toronto's best hidden gems. Splendid during the fall but it offers a great walk at any time of the year. One thing leading to another, I also discovered how to hop from one little park to another to explore the area, with a chance to stroll through Toronto's whimsical gay village.

STROLL 11

Toronto area
DOWNTOWN

Neighbourhood
Church-Wellesley

Full loop
6.2 km (9,540 steps)

Time estimate
1 hr 35 min

Mindset
When you are in
the mood for a little
adventure to discover
the city's hidden
shortcuts.

Subway & TTC
• Exit at **Sherbourne
Subway Station**.
• You can exit at
**Bloor-Yonge Sub-
way Station** and start
the loop at #10, or exit
at **College Subway
Station** and start at
#12.

Best parking
• Go on **Best Parking
app** (www.bestpark-
ing.com) and search
**Sherbourne Subway
Station.**

Nathalie's TIPS
• See p. 95 for more
tips to help you plan
this walk.

First things first

1 One block west of
**Sherbourne Subway
Station** is **Eggspectation**,
a good meeting point for
a big breakfast (they open
at 7 am).

2 For a caffeine fix,
consider off-the-beat-
en-track **Rooster Coffee
House**, a cool café with
mezzanine, sitting pretty on
Jarvis St in front of a major
blue piece of public art.

3 From **Eggspectation**,
cross Bloor St E and
look for the stairs just west
of the bridge to walk down
to Mt Pleasant Rd. (If you
are coming from **Rooster
Coffee House**, cross
Charles St and walk down
Mt Pleasant Rd.)

4 Either way, you'll
reach the impressive
murals of seasonal land-
scapes on both sides of Mt
Pleasant's underpass, done
by Ian Leventhal in 2006.

5 Walk a bit further to
admire Rosedale Val-
ley Rd from the bridge!

6 Climb back to Bloor St
E, using the stairs at 74
Mt Pleasant Rd, and go westbound. You will reach one
of my favourite sculptures in
Toronto: *Community* by Kirk
Newman. (Take a minute to
enjoy the humour in the lively
crowd where playing kids
mingle with businessmen
with cell phones.)

Across the street is
**St. Paul's Bloor Street
Church**, one of Toronto's
finest examples of integration of old and new architecture. (If you have a chance,
go inside. The main chapel
features gorgeous stained
glass windows. So do the
washrooms!)

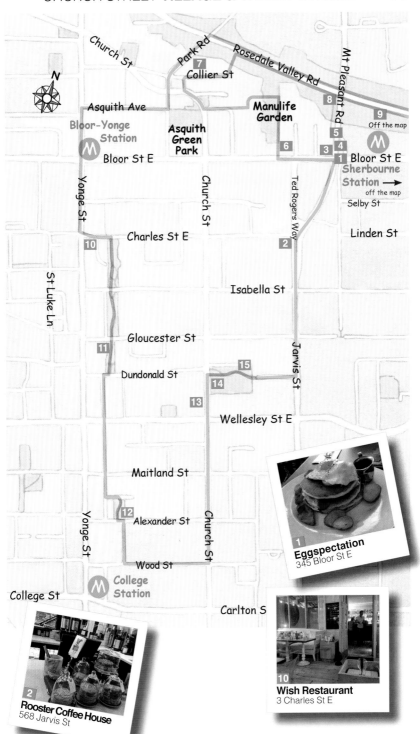

1 Eggspectation
345 Bloor St E

2 Rooster Coffee House
568 Jarvis St

10 Wish Restaurant
3 Charles St E

You should be able to enter the **Manulife Garden** near the sculpture (on the east side of the **Manulife Financial Headquarters**). It exits into St. Paul's Square.

Rosedale Valley

St. Paul"s Square becomes Asquith Ave. Turn right on Church St and right again in the lane you will find to your right, past the **Milner Parkette**. It will get you to secluded Collier St.

7 I especially like accessing the **Rosedale Ravine** from the long staircase in this quiet dead-end. So country-like!

Few pedestrians walk the long and winding ravine street, which is in fact a busy boulevard masquerading as a country road.

A sidewalk runs over 2 kms along the south side of Rosedale Valley Rd, from Park Rd to Bayview Ave, further east.

The road is towered over by tall trees, which makes for a spectacular panorama in the fall. At other times, it is still unique enough to be visited.

8 As you go eastbound, you will walk under the **Mt Pleasant Road Bridge** (with a long staircase allowing you to return to Mt Pleasant Rd and, one flight of stairs higher, to Bloor St E).

Further east, you'll pass the Sherbourne St N Bridge, followed by the **Glen Road Pedestrian Bridge**. (Wondering how people access this? Off **Sherbourne Subway Station**, by exiting into Glen Rd, on the east side of the station.)

9 Then, you'll walk under the covered arch of **Rosedale Valley Bridge**, followed by an impressive bridge dated 1919, which is actually an extension of the imposing **Prince Edward Viaduct** linking Bloor St to Danforth Ave, further east.

On your way back, turn left at Park Rd. Can you see the wolf in the small **Asquith Green Park** to your left? Turn right on Asquith Ave to Yonge St.

Yonge Street

On your right, is **Toronto Reference Library**, one of Toronto's largest libraries, quite a sight with its curving atrium and soothing fountain. You'll find an effervescent **Balzac's Café** inside, at street level.

10 Turn left on Yonge St, then left again at Charles St. I have stopped many times at **Wish Restaurant** for a bite or a glass of wine (or both). I can't resist its rustic cottage appeal. Make sure to check their beautiful wooden panels inside.

A bit further to your right, turn into **George Hislop Park**. It serves as a green shortcut used by locals to avoid busy Yonge St.

11 Keep going southbound past Isabella St and Gloucester St through **James Canning Gardens**.

Turn right to find the narrow Chechalk Ln. Keep going southbound. Beyond Wellesley St E, it becomes Maitland Terrace.

Past Maitland St, look for Sky Gilbert Ln to your left, to access **Alexander Street Parkette**.

12 This lovely little park faces the entrance to popular **Buddies in Bad Times Theatre**, presenting edgy shows since 1979.

Church Street

Continue down the lane across Alexander St (passing along the **Marriott Hotel**) and turn left at Wood St.

The art installation running along Wood St and nearby Reverend Porter Ln was commissioned by the **Toronto Hydro Corporation**. It represents a timeline of the evolution of Hydro from 1910 to 2015.

13 Turn left at Church St, the heart of the city's gay village, peppered with omnipresent rainbows and lively with bars and clubs offering drag performances and trivia nights, such as very popular **Crews & Tangos**, adorned with a great mural by Elicser.

Church St is actually graced with eleven murals capturing some of **Church-Wellesley Village** and Toronto's LGBTQ history, with the **BMO Bank of Montreal** as a partner. They were commissioned in 2014, when Toronto was hosting **WorldPride**.

14 Walk to **Barbara Hall Park**, north of Wellesley St E, to see one of Toronto's most welcoming squares, with checkered cobbled stones and the beautiful artwork by Christiano De Araujo.

15 Go further into the park to visit the **AIDS Memorial**. Then continue into Cawthra Square, and turn left at Jarvis St.

NATHALIE'S **TIPS TO PLAN** THIS STROLL

For a shorter walk

Even in the shorter version of this stroll, there is the possibility to enjoy both VILLAGE and VALLEY! The following 2.7-km oop (42-min walk) follows #1 to #5. Then, instead of using the stairs at 74 Pleasant Rd to climb back to Bloor St E, you will take the stairs going down into the ravine (see #8). Walk westbound to admire Rosedale Valley Rd, and watch for stairs on your left (see #7), before you reach Park Rd. Go up to Collier St and turn left on Park Rd, and right at Asquith Ave to Yonge St. You can then read the Yonge Street description on page 93 up to #11. Past **James Canning Gardens**, turn left on Dundonald St to Church St. Cross the street to go through the welcoming square of **Barbara Hall Park** (see #14 and #15) and turn left at Jarvis St to complete the loop.

About timing and logistics

• See the **Pride Toronto**'s website **www.pridetoronto.com** to learn about the Pride festival, including **Pride Parade**, Canada's biggest LGBTQ event running later in June along Yonge St with side activities on Church St turned carless for the occasion.

Romantic mood

• My favourite romantic combo around this stroll would be a great movie at **Cineplex Cinemas Varsity** (in the **Manulife Centre**, 55 Bloor St W), followed by a glass of wine at the quaint cottage-like patio of **Wish** (see #10). Note that their kitchen will probably be closed by the time you arrive after a late show but their bar should still be open. Consult the **Varsity**'s movie listing at **www.cinemaclock.com**.

Family fun

• You can easily play an *I Spy animal* game with your kids when admiring the two murals on Mount Pleasant Rd (see #4). There are so many of them!

A little extra in the area

• Check the mini-walk #19 on page 227 in the last chapter **#torontourbangems**.

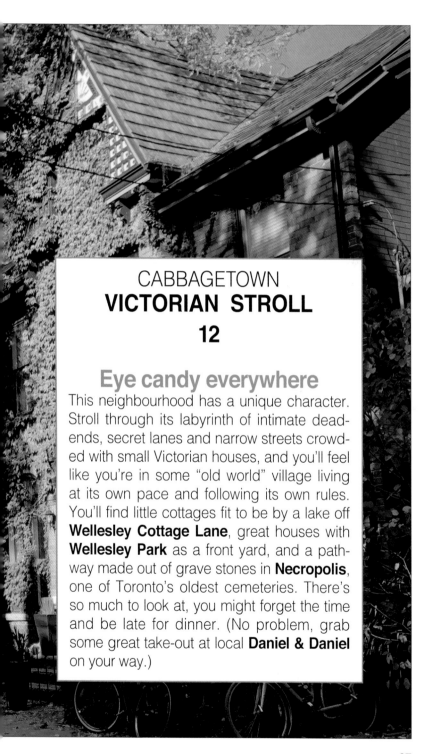

CABBAGETOWN
VICTORIAN STROLL
12

Eye candy everywhere

This neighbourhood has a unique character. Stroll through its labyrinth of intimate dead-ends, secret lanes and narrow streets crowded with small Victorian houses, and you'll feel like you're in some "old world" village living at its own pace and following its own rules. You'll find little cottages fit to be by a lake off **Wellesley Cottage Lane**, great houses with **Wellesley Park** as a front yard, and a pathway made out of grave stones in **Necropolis**, one of Toronto's oldest cemeteries. There's so much to look at, you might forget the time and be late for dinner. (No problem, grab some great take-out at local **Daniel & Daniel** on your way.)

STROLL 12

Toronto area
DOWNTOWN

Neighbourhood
Cabbagetown

Full loop
(5.5 km (8,460 steps)

Time estimate
1 hr 25 min

Mindset
When you want to be surrounded by man-made beauty and feel warm and fuzzy inside.

Subway & TTC
• Streetcar **506**, bus **65**.

Best parking
• Go on **Best Parking app** (www.bestpark-ing.com) and search **JetFuel Coffee**.

Nathalie's TIPS
• See p. 103 for more tips to help you plan this walk.

First things first

1 If you're just craving great coffee, **JetFuel Coffee Shop** is a must (and a good meeting point). Their foamy lattes are delicious. They open daily at 6 am and if you show up before 11 am, they should still have tasty pastries left.

Closer to lunch time? I love the café's neighbour, **Salt & Tobacco** for the best mushroom pizza ever. A fantastic addition to **Cabbagetown**.

2 If you'd rather sit for breakfast, **Johnny G's** is an honest all-day breakfast restaurant with vintage vibes, still holding the fort. Best options are the traditional bacon & egg or Eggs Benedict.

Country-like

3 Go to Carlton St, east of Parliament St, and turn right through Dermott Place, for a true small town feel.

4 Turn left on Spruce St, left on Sackville St, then right on Carlton St and left again on Bowman St to see cute Sackville Pl and, turning right, Rawlings Ave, which sits between two gorgeous ivy-covered houses at Carlton St.

5 Go south on Sumach St and back to luscious Spruce St (simply gorgeous under the summer morning light) walk east, to the end of Spruce St, into a country-like section you can't access by car.

Take the path to your left. (**Riverdale Park West** is expanding to your right.) Turn left onto Geneva Ave for your first close look at Cabbagetown's little row houses.

Johnny G's
478 Parliament St

JetFuel Coffee Shop
519 Parliament St

Salt & Tobacco
521 Parliament St

6 Then, turn right on Sumach St, and right again into Gordon Sinclair Lane, especially pretty in the fall.

Sumach Street

Going north towards **Riverdale Park** and **Farm**, can you see the raccoon sculpture?

7 Walk to Sumach St to admire some of the most beautiful houses in Cabbagetown. (These owners sure know how to maintain a house!)

8 At Winchester, turn right to enter the **Necropolis Cemetery**, one of the oldest cemeteries in Toronto. Follow the road to your right and walk straight, where it curves, until you reach section **R**.

9 To your left, you'll see the most bucolic scene: two stone trails lined with memorial plates, sheltered by the trees.

They will lead to the main loop and back to the entrance of the cemetery, where you'll turn right to get to Sumach St.

Stroll ahead to Amelia St, then turn right to access **Wellesley Park**, a little gem of a park hidden from the street.

Wellesley Park

10 See the houses facing this park on the south side? No street, no sidewalk. **Wellesley Park** is their front yard!

A winding path runs through the park. The long staircase in the northeast corner leads down to Rosedale Valley Rd (a must see during fall colours).

Wellesley Street

Every road going north from Wellesley St E is worth visiting! Most of them are dead-end streets, some with little dirt paths to access the next.

Turn right on Parkview Ave and walk to the end. You'll find a dirt road. (Who would have expected this sight in urban Toronto?)

Take it to reach St. James Ct. Then return to Wellesley St E and turn right onto Wellesley Ave. This dead-end street is special. It ends with a touching plate erected in memory of a fellow resident who died in the 90s. (A very nice man who lives on that street told me about this neighbour.)

11 The next road west is Sackville St. Walk to the end to check this other lovely cul-de-sac and look into the cute Alpha Ave. Then return to Wellesley St E and turn right into Wellesley Cottages.

12 At the turn, you will see the little cottages giving the street its name. They look like dollhouses. Last time I visited, you could read the following on a little tongue-in-cheek sign posted on the white picket fence: *In 1832 on this spot nothing happened.*

You can then walk west through a small path to access Laurier Ave. Back on Wellesley St, turn right then take Iroquois Lane to your left.

Around the corner, the Italian family restaurant on Amelia St is called **F'Amelia**. Get it?

Parliament Street

Walk west on Amelia S to Parliament St, and turn left to see a cluster of coo shops.

The selection a **Blooming Flower Ba** (559 Parliament St) is gor geous. Next door, **MHC Vintage** has an interest ing spread of clothes Further south, **Menagerie Pet Shop** has great curb appeal with its giant lizard on the facade.

Across the street a Winchester St is the bril liant shop run by residentia designers **Kendall & Co** (514 Parliament St).

Metcalfe Street

Go east on Winchester S and turn left at Metcalfe St You'll walk by the historic **Toronto Dance Theatre** (a former church).

13 The large house a Metcalfe St & Salis bury Ave is impressive There's a cozy feeling to the rest of Salisbury Ave (especially when Christmas lights are up).

At Sackville St, turr right, then right again into Winchester St. Turn left a Metcalfe St to see all kinds of architectural detail Then take Carlton St to your right to Parliament St.

A drink (and swee potato fries) at the charming bistro **House on Parliament** (454 Parliament St) would be a nice end to this walk.

14 But before, stop a **Labour of Love** (223 Carlton St). This whimsica shop has a fantastic assort ment of gift ideas, books and cards. And wait till you see their jewelry selection!

NATHALIE'S **TIPS TO PLAN** THIS STROLL

For a shorter walk
The part of this stroll one should not miss is Wellesley St with its dead-end side streets, and **Wellesley Park**. The following 2.6 km loop (40-min walk) covers it all. From Parliament St, go east on Winchester St and turn left on Metcalfe St to get to the heart of **Cabbagetown**, at the corner of Metcalfe St & Salisbury Ave (see #13). Go along Salisbury St, then turn right at Sackville St and left at Winchester to reach Sumach St. Turn left and stroll ahead to Amelia St, and turn right to access **Wellesley Park**. Follow #10 to #12. Turn left on Parliament St (see page 102), and back to Winchester St.

About timing and logistics
• The **Cabbagetown Festival** is a most popular fall event held in **Riverdale Park** and surroundings on the weekend following the Labour Day long weekend. See **www.cabbagetownfestival.ca** for details.

Romantic mood
• You can grab everything for a fancy picnic at the French caterer **Daniel et Daniel** with a storefront at 248 Carlton St and go to the vast **Wellesley Park** to find a quiet spot (bring a blanket!).
• An evening candlelit dinner at the outdoor patio of intimate Italian restaurant **F'Amelia** (12 Amelia St) on a warm summer night is in great danger of turning you into *Lady and the Tramp* Disney characters.

Family fun
• Ask your kids to find the wooden raccoon in **Riverdale Park** near the farm. (Hint: it is closer to Carlton St... and the cow paddock.)
• You will find all the details about **Riverdale Farm** (across from # 8) at **www.riverdalefarmtoronto.ca**. Did you know it is a real working farm?
• The **Forsythia Festival** is an utterly cute parade celebrating spring and the blossoming of the yellow forsythia (there are many in the neighbourhood). It is organized by the **Cabbagetown Residents Association**, inviting everyone to wear yellow and decorate their bikes with anything yellow: balloons, flowers, ribbons, etc. The crowd gathers at 10 am on the first Sunday in May, at Winchester St & Sumach St, and march along the streets, ending with festivities in **Wellesley Park** until 3 pm. This great family fun has been a tradition for almost 50 years! See **www.cabbagetowner.com** to see their photo gallery.

A little extra in the area
• Check the mini-walk #18 on page 226 in the last chapter **#torontourbangems**.

EVERGREEN
BRICK WORKS STROLL
13

Oasis in the city

You can do this stroll the easy way. Just park your car in one of the large parking lots on site (or catch the free shuttle from **Broadview Subway Station**) and go straight to the **Farmers' Market** or the **Café Belong** to gorge on yummy food, then casually walk on the boardwalk overlooking the marsh... Or you can make it more challenging, arriving on foot from the ravine path connecting to **Evergreen Brick Works** on either side of the site. (This way, you'll really deserve those scrumptious treats from the café or the market!)

STROLL
13

Toronto area
MIDTOWN

Neighbourhood
Rosedale

Full loop
4.2 km (6,460 steps)

Time estimate
1 hr 05 min

Mindset
When you're in a "green" mindset, thirsty for nature and hope for better cities.

Subway & TTC
• Catch a free shuttle bus to **Evergreen** from the parkette just north of **Broadview Subway Station**.

Best parking
• You can park on the premises for $6.
• There's plenty of free street parking along Douglas Drive (north of **Chorley Park**) and on nearby streets north of Douglas. You can then start the loop at #13, going backwards.

Nathalie's TIPS
• See p. 111 for more tips to help you plan this walk.

First things first

A decade ago, we needed to see the bricks mingle with the sand and pebbles on the paths to remind us there was a brick factory for a whole century on this site. Not anymore.

1 Thanks to the massive development project managed by **Evergreen**, all deteriorating heritage buildings have been salvaged and integrated into an exciting showcase of urban green design, with the watershed sculpture as a centrepiece in the **Tiffany Commons**.

2 The lovely patio is tempting but it is reserved to the patrons of the foodie restaurant of **Café Belong**. Luckily, you can stop at its **Grab & Go** counter next door, for great coffee, scrumptious treats and light fare; an excellent meeting point.

Across from the **Grab & Go** is the wonderful **Evergreen Garden Market**, filled with original gift ideas, preserves, books and gardening items.

3 At the end of the hall is the door to the **Koerner Gardens** with skating rink weekends and Holidays, weather permitting (now featuring a laid back café with alcohol permit).

4 The building next door has been turned into the **TD Future Cities Centre**. Bad news: the historic kilns are now accessible on weekends only. Very good news: on weekends from 10 am to 3 pm, the Centre opens its doors to the public to enjoy the very cool *Future Cities Exhibits*.

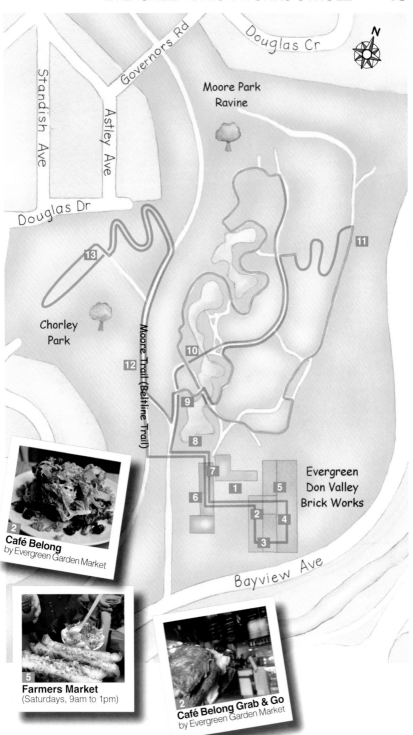

Douglas Cr

N

Governors Rd

Standish Ave

Astley Ave

Moore Park
Ravine

Douglas Dr

13

11

Chorley
Park

Moore Trail (Beltine Trail)

12

10

9

8

7

1

6

2

5

Evergreen
Don Valley
Brick Works

2

4

3

2
Café Belong
by Evergreen Garden Market

5
Farmers Market
(Saturdays, 9am to 1pm)

Bayview Ave

2
Café Belong Grab & Go
by Evergreen Garden Market

5 With the help of light effects, multimedia and pertinent displays over the original structures, this exhibition transforms the space into a slick post-industrial think-tank of what makes a flourishing city.

6 Return by the **Tiffany Commons** and walk north through **The Pavilions**. This is where you'll find the year-round **Farmers Market** on Saturdays from 9 am to 1 pm (it actually moves indoors from early November to spring).

Amidst the usual organic fruit and vegetables and craft offerings, expect delicious breakfasts and lunches to go, great coffee, beer and plenty of other treats.

7 As you exit into the wilderness, you pass wonderful iron panels with animal cutouts.

Brick Works Trails

Even with all the developments in the last 10 years, **Evergreen Brick Works** still feels like a precious enclave hidden in the big mega city.

8 In the summer, whole sections of the pond are filled with water lilies. We can often see cranes by the water and those who are patient enough might glimpse a snapping turtle.

9 Walk on the platform west of the pond and follow the wider path into the wide-open space and to the end of the old quarry. (Don't be afraid to explore every nook. The park isn't so big that you could get lost!)

We could mistake the walls of the quarry for a natural escarpment shielding us from the urban noise. Hard to imagine that it was a industrial site for nearly 100 years, producing 25 million bricks a year at its peak!

10 Complete the loop, walking through the boardwalk into a paved path running up the hill.

At the highest point, take the narrow path on your left to access the belvedere offering a grand panorama of the site with the **CN Tower** in the background.

11 Follow the trail along the edge of the old quarry for another great view of the meandering path around the pond.

Then walk down the paved path and return to the platform by the pond.

Chorley Park

12 Take the trail going west of the platform to access the portion of the **Beltline Trail** that many still call the **Moore Trail**. (**Mount Pleasant Cemetery** is less than 30 min up that trail.)

13 There used to be a steep dirt path taking us up from the trail to **Chorley Park**. The City has replaced it with a serpentine path in 2019.

This means that the option of parking for free on the streets near Chorley Park is now accessible to everyone.

Going back down this paved path, turn right on the **Beltline Trail** to return to **Evergreen Brick Works** in 5 minutes.

NATHALIE'S **TIPS TO PLAN** THIS STROLL

For a shorter walk

If you drop the walk up the belvedere (on the eastern side of the park) and up **Chorley Park** (on the western side) you will get a comfortable 2.1-km loop (30-min walk) without losing the chance to enjoy the beautiful ponds of **Evergreen Brick Works**, where one truly gets a delightful moment of escape.

About timing and logistics

• The free Evergreen shuttle bus departs every 30–45 minutes from the parkette on Erindale Ave (just north of **Broadview Subway Station**). It will also take you back to the subway station for free (last departure at 7 pm). You'll find the bus schedule on **www.evergreen.ca** in the *Visitor Info* under *Evergreen Brick Works* tab. Note that there are only 20 seats on the bus.

• The **Saturday Farmers Market** (see #6) is Toronto's largest farmers' market, offering the widest variety of local and seasonal food in the city. It runs year-round on Saturdays from 9 am to 1 pm. (NOTE that it moves indoors from November to spring near #3.)

• The indoor **Evergreen Garden Market** is open year-round from 10 am to 6 pm on weekdays, from 9 am to 5 pm on Saturdays and 10 am to 5 pm on Sundays and Holidays.

• The **Sunday Artisans Market** runs from May to November on Sundays from 10 am to 3 pm in the same pavilion as the Saturday market (see #6). It includes artisans as well as food merchants.

• The *Future Cities Exhibits* is free and open Saturday and Sunday from 10 am to 3 pm (see #5).

Romantic mood

• The casual post-industrial look of **Café Belong** with two full walls of bay windows is warm and beautiful. The lovely outdoor patio is for the exclusive use of the restaurant's patrons. The food is exquisite, expensive, but presented in decent portions. They do lunches, dinner and weekend brunches. You could indulge yourself with a 3-course chef's choice with wine pairing, for $110. A treat for special occasions.

Family fun

• The **Children's Garden** is a wonderful space filled with natural play elements, on the north side of the buildings, under the tall chimney. It is open year-round on weekends, from 10 am to 4 pm in summertime, 1 am to 3 pm in wintertime, and 11 am to 3 pm on Holidays. Suggested donation of $5 per child.

A little extra in the area

• Check the mini-walk #51 on page 243 in the last chapter **#torontourbangems**.

ROSEDALE
MEANDERING STROLL
14

The "crème de la crème"

There's more to this delightful stroll amidst one of Toronto's wealthiest neighbourhoods than meets the eye. It includes the prettiest access to the **Beltline Trail**, via the **Cat's Eye Bridge**, and **Mount Pleasant Cemetery** (one of Toronto's best parks), a pedestrian bridge offering a lovely view over surprising streets with a true countryside feel. On the only commercial stretch in this residential area, you'll find **Dolce Bakery** selling pastries, coffee and chocolates (to start you on the right foot) and the fabulous **Summerhill Market** with fine grocery and take-out of all kinds (for a big finish before heading home).

STROLL
14

Toronto area
MIDTOWN

Neighbourhood
Rosedale
+ Moore Park

Full loop
5.6 km (8,615 steps)

Time estimate
1 hr 25 min

Mindset
When you want the simple pleasure of a countryside vibe AND the posh indulgence of a decadent treat.

Subway & TTC
• Bus **82**.

Best parking
• There is free street parking around **Summerhill Market** and nearby streets. I find it easier to find parking spots after 10 a.m. north of Summerhill Avenue (accessible from Carstowe Rd).

Nathalie's TIPS
• See p. 119 for more tips to help you plan this walk.

First things first

1 A visit to cute **Dolce Bakery** is a good start to this walk, for good coffee... and a "bombe" doughnut or a decadent Gewürztraminer ball (yummy!).

2 Walk west to climb the ramp crossing over the train tracks. Make sure you look east over the tracks to catch a genuine country sight.

MacLennan Avenue

3 On the other side of the tracks, walk down the stairs and around the corner to your right.

4 Isn't Carstowe Rd bucolic? The first time I saw this street, I just couldn't believe I was in Canada's biggest city.

5 Then, go up MacLennan Ave. The mural on the wall has seen better days but I find it charming. (Many boho cafés would kill for that kind of vintage look!)

Keep going north to Inglewood Dr, where you turn right, then left onto Welland Ave.

Heath Street East

6 On Heath St E, turn right to reach the pedestrian bridge passing over the **Moore Park Ravine Trail** and **Mud Creek**. It is called the **Cat's Eye Bridge**. When you look at it at a certain angle, you get the idea.

Everything around this passage is lovely in the summer, but it becomes truly spectacular when all the leaves are in full colour.

Dolce Bakery
420 Summerhill Ave

Summerhill Market
446 Summerhill Ave

Heath Street East

7 Once you've crossed the bridge, turn left and follow the path down to reach the trail, where you'll turn right.

Note that if you turned left on the trail, you would reach **Evergreen Brick Works** in about 15 minutes, following the **Beltline Trail**.

Moore Park Ravine

8 Along the way, when you have a chance, have a look at the river running down the ravine.

The trees provide a most welcome shade in the heat of the summer.

Across the street, you'll reach **Mount Pleasant Cemetery**. The Moore entrance is not accessible by car but a bike trail runs through this entrance, the closest to the **Visitation Centre**.

Into the cemetery

9 By the Centre's parking lot, is the entrance to the **Forest of Remembrance**, where mature trees tower over natural rocks bearing memorial plates.

It will take you to the iron gate of **Section 22**, beyond which await two graceful geese in flight and the romantic sculpture of an embracing couple.

10 Further, you'll reach the **Garden of Remembrance** with beautifully landscaped pond and running stream around the **Columbarium**.

The attention to detail is quite impressive all around, down to the bike racks! They look like pieces of art for a good reason. They are the winning design of a Bicycle Rack Design Competition held in 2010 by **Ryerson University** with **Mount Pleasant Cemetery**.)

11 Brace yourself on your way back to the forest. There's a whole section of plaques for infants infused with the resigned pain of broken-hearted parents. Hard not to cry...

Hudson Drive

Walk back to the trail across Moore Ave and the **Cat's Eye Bridge**. On the other end of the bridge, turn left on Hudson Dr, for a taste of the **Rosedale** neighbourhood.

Keep to your left at St. Clair Ave E, it becomes Harper Ave at the turn. Check the lovely dead-ends of Harper Gardens and Valley View to your left.

Then turn left again on Inglewood Dr. It becomes Rosedale Heights Dr, which you'll follow until you reach MacLennan Ave.

12 It is worth making a left into Old Bridle Path. This country-like dead-end seems frozen in time.

Then it's back over the pedestrian bridge to **Summerhill Market**.

13 The same way one would not expect such a quaint country feeling in posh Rosedale, one would not think she would find such a trendy market in the middle of this residential area.

There's quite a spread in the upscale grocery store. Time for a take-out dinner!

NATHALIE'S **TIPS TO PLAN** THIS STROLL

For a shorter walk
This stroll is all about the delight of discovering country charm in Canada's biggest urban area. The following 2.2-km loop (35-min walk) will make you forget you are in Toronto, except for the part where you'll check out **Summerhill Market**. This has posh Toronto written all over it! Simply follow #1 to #4, push it to the end of Carstowe Rd, then go to #5. Finally, walk uphill to see #12, then return to #1.

About timing and logistics
• The bus stop is right at the foot of the stairs crossing over the train track (see #2).
• There are 1-hr street-parking spots around the market. If you would rather take your time, I recommend doing the walk after 10 am to find street parking on the roads north of the track. You can access them from Carstowe Rd.
• Check **Summerhill Market** online at **www.summerhillmarket.com** to see the vast spread they carry. I always take advantage of this stroll to buy a take-out dinner (which I did not have to cook from scratch because I was too busy enjoying this walk with my girlfriends).

Romantic mood
• Bring a blanket, grab a picnic at **Summerhill Market** (see #13), chocolates at **Dolce Bakery** (see #1), and find the best spot under the tall trees along Carstowne Rd (see #4).

Family fun
• Tell the kids about the **Cat's Eye Bridge** (see #6), then let them wrap their brain around that as you walk there. It is my favourite part of this stroll to visit with kids. It has everything a young adventurer could wish for: bridge, stairs, creek, sheltered trail.

A little extra in the area
• It's only while preparing this guide that I realized that Summerhill Ave becomes Douglas Dr and runs along **Chorley Park**, 200 metres east of **Summerhill Market**! It is my favourite way to access **Evergreen Brick Works** (see page 104).

MOUNT PLEASANT
CEMETERY STROLL
15

The long and winding road...

If you want to be surrounded by beauty, **Mount Pleasant Cemetery**'s picturesque stroll is for you. You won't feel like an intruder in this resting place, also a favourite amongst cyclists and joggers who use its winding paths. From the beginning (in 1876), this cemetery was designed after the 19th Century tradition of rural cemeteries and intended as a place of recreation and contemplation. Mount Pleasant features such a variety of trees that it qualifies as one of the biggest arboretums in Canada. No wonder the park-like cemetery is so splendid in the fall, especially on a bright sunny day.

STROLL
15

Toronto area
MIDTOWN

Neighbourhood
Deer Park

Full loop
7.6 km (11,690 steps)

Time estimate
1 hr 55 min

Mindset
When you want to be gently reminded of the inescapable Circle of Life and the actual privilege of being alive.

Subway & TTC
• Exit at **St. Clair Subway Station** and take a 6-min walk northbound on Yonge St.

Best parking
• If you use the parking lot by the **Visitation Centre** as a starting point (adjacent to section **25**), start the walk at #10.
• Go on **Best Parking app** (www.bestparking.com) and search **Mount Pleasant Cemetery**.

Nathalie's TIPS
• See p. 127 for more tips to help you plan this walk.

First things first

1 You can grab an excellent coffee at **JJ Bean Coffee Roasters**, not far from **St. Clair Subway Station**, on St. Clair Ave W, just west of Yonge.

While you're there, facing south, look up! There is one of Toronto's tallest murals. The giant is a creation of UK-based street artist Phlegm.

2 **Mary Be Kitchen**, right by the mural, is a great option for breakfast or lunch, with a lovely fresh decor and delicious healthy food (on weekdays, their breakfast menu is offered from 8 to 11:15 am).

Walk around the west side of **Mary Be** to the back. You will get a better view of the giant. Can you spot the **CN Tower** in the details?

Past the metal staircase, a narrow corridor takes you to Yonge St. On your right, a couple of doors down, sits **Zelden's Deli and Desserts**, which could be a good place to stop after the walk (polaroid #2 on map). Open 9 am to 9 pm, they make their own pastrami, serve Jewish traditional fare and more. When we were there, there were lots of funny little signs to read, such as "Be a mensch, let her have the bench."

Cross at the lights on St. Clair and walk northbound on Yonge St to the **Mount Pleasant Cemetery**. Spanning over 205 acres, it was opened in 1876.

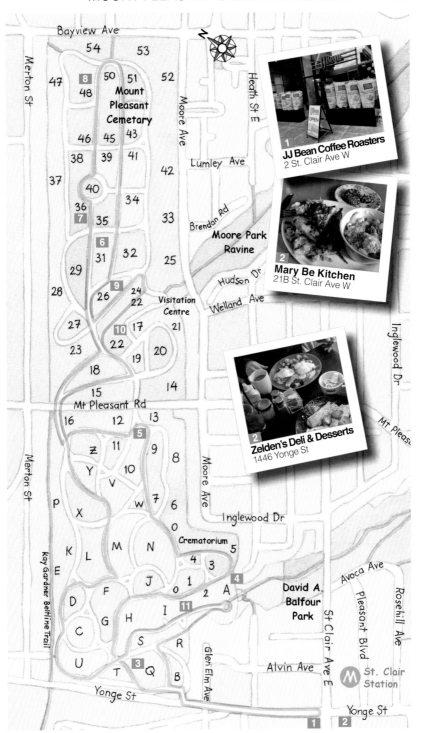

JJ Bean Coffee Roasters
2 St. Clair Ave W

Mary Be Kitchen
21B St. Clair Ave W

Zelden's Deli & Desserts
1446 Yonge St

About the sections

Each section of **Mount Pleasant Cemetery** is identified with a letter or a number, nailed to a tree, relatively well in sight. Map in hand, you'll always know where you are. (There are 12 km of paved paths in this park!)

Sections T & Q

3 After entering at the Yonge entrance, turn left. Then stroll between **T** and **Q**, where the French mausoleum faces a symmetrical garden.

Walk up along **G** and **F**. (See the little boys, and the valley behind?)

4 Between **J** and **H**, take the right fork to access section **2** where a line-up of mausoleums await including the Eaton family's, impressive with its wrap-around columns and guardian lions.

Then, turn right, around the **Crematorium** and the two beautiful women. Walk between **N** and **O** and keep going with Sections **7**, **9**, and **13** on your right.

5 You'll see Alexander the Great on a horse on the imposing monument by the Mount Pleasant entrance. It marks the tomb of Steve Stavro, at one point the owner of the Toronto Maple Leafs team and the Toronto Raptors.

Follow the road between **11** and **12** past this monument, and turn right, to go through the tunnel running under Mount Pleasant Rd.

Note that the iron gates to your left opens into the **Beltline Trail**.

Sections 23 & 18

Walk between **23** and **18** and turn left around **23**. Keep going between **29** and **31**.

6 On your right, you'll see the poetic statue of a man holding a bird.

7 Across, in **36**, can you find the giant religious icon, near a loyal dog by a grave?

Along the way, you'll notice many Chinese markers including a life-size family in section **39**.

8 Section **48** on your left features low walls which give this part the feel of an English country field. Look it up on Google Satellite; they form a cross!

9 Turn right around **50**, into the pretty path between **51** and **50**. Keep going, past sections **33** and **32**. In section **26** on your left, look for the amazing sculpture of the *Devine Servant*.

Visitation Centre

Walk southbound on the road between **22** and **26**. Turn right around section **24** and find the green gate of the **Forest of Remembrance**, a peaceful resting place with plaques on rocks

Brace yourself for what lies beyond, to your left. This is the ground where babies are buried...

10 Then walk past the stone fountain, down into the beautiful **Garden of Remembrance** with a vast reflecting pool, a stream, a rockery and gorgeous landscaping.

Sections 18 & 15

At the other end of the garden, walk down the road between sections **18** and **15** and through the tunnel.

You'll emerge into the picturesque road along section **16**, on your left.

Sections X & Y

Between **X** and **Y**, the *Tree of Life* on your left is one of the few modern artworks here.

Keep strolling between **M** and **L** and you'll get to admire the intricate work on the Massey family mausoleum, designed by the architect who did **Casa Loma** and old **City Hall**.

Sections D & E

Go right, around **L**, and stroll between **D** and **E**. Further west, past the pedestrian entrance, you'll face the temple-like Thomson mausoleum.

Follow the curved path running along the bucolic section **U**. Go straight towards **Q** and take the fork left of section **S**, disappearing amidst the trees.

Section S

Walk between the gravestones on your left. That's where you'll find the bronze of a golfer, probably the tribute of a loving wife.

At the turn of the road around **S**, you'll see on your left the original sculpture of two young firemen forever playing with a ladder. Then, it's **R** and **B**, back to the entrance.

NATHALIE'S **TIPS TO PLAN** THIS STROLL

For a shorter walk

For a shorter walk, stick to the part of the cemetery located west of Mount Pleasant Rd for a 2.9-km loop. Follow #3 to #5 but don't go through the tunnel, turn left and walk between sections **X** and **Y**, then **M** and **L**, and **D** and **E** (follow the descriptions on page 126). Finally, follow the curved path running along section **U,** and back to the Yonge entrance. Note that you are allowed to park within the cemetery and have a little walk around your favourite section described in this guide.

About timing and logistics

• To download a map of the cemetery, go to **www.mountpleasantgroup. com/en-CA/Locations/Cemeteries/Mount-Pleasant**. You can also get a printed map at the office within the **Funeral Centre** (south of #10).

• The gates open at 8 am and close at 8 pm in summertime, and 5:30 pm in wintertime. The office is closed on Sundays and public holidays.

Romantic mood

• The **Garden of Remembrance** (see #10) is beautiful and relaxing, with a few benches and the gentle sounds of the fountain.

Family fun

• Ask your kids to spot the **CN Tower** in Phlem's mural (see #2).

• Such a large variety of trees can be found in this cemetery that it is considered one of North America's most significant arboretums. During the fall, it becomes a great harvesting ground for your leaf collectors.

• You can ask your kids to look for art depicting a specific theme: angels, animals, children, family crests. It is perfectly OK to walk on the grass!

• After reading a few dates written on gravestones with your kids, you will be able to discuss with them the random nature of death. Here, parents bid farewell to their child; there a woman said good-bye to her husband; farther away, a whole family was buried a long time ago. Some tombstones even show a picture of the deceased, for a more concrete experience. Fertile ground for conversation, indeed!

• Make sure to show your kids the dog watching over his master (see #7).

A little extra in the area

• Check the mini-walk #21 on page 228 in the last chapter **#torontourbangems**.

• You could continue your walk north of the cemetery with the *Forest Hill BELTLINE Stroll* (see page 137, #6).

CASA LOMA
STAIRCASE STROLL
16

Move over Stairmaster!

For years, I visited **Casa Loma** with my kids without realizing Toronto's most impressive staircase lies at the foot of a little park just east of the castle. It offers a great view of Spadina Road... and of personal trainers torturing poor clients huffing and puffing up and down the stairs, casually suggesting "One more, two steps" to the red-faced client as she runs by while he stands watching. No need to run if you don't want to but this stroll also includes the staircase under Spadina, the one down **Nordheimer Ravine**, two more around **Sir Winston Churchill Park**, and a coffee break.

STROLL 16

Toronto area
MIDTOWN

Neighbourhood
**Casa Loma
+ South Hill**

Full loop
5.2 km (8,000 steps)

Time estimate
1 hr 20 min

Mindset
When you want to let off some steam and get a nice workout (without even realizing it).

Subway & TTC
• Exit at **Dupont Subway Station** (or exit at **St. Clair West** and start the loop at #7).

Best parking
• It's easier on weekends to find street parking for more than 2 hours. Parking at **Casa Loma** or **George Brown College** costs around $10.
• Go on **Best Parking app** (www.bestparking.com) and search **Casa Loma**.

Nathalie's TIPS
• See p. 135 for more tips to help you plan this walk.

First things first

1 My new favourite way to start this stroll is at **Belle's Bakery**, around the corner from **Dupont Subway Station**. Open at 7:30 am on weekdays, a bit later on the weekends, it is a great meeting point with seating.

Expect chocolate croissants, almond croissant, brioche egg cups, mini quiches and good coffee.

2 If you'd rather have lunch (and cocktails), before or after the walk, look no further than Middle eastern **Fet Zun**, for its delicious sharing plates, spreads, Israeli breakfast, pistachio halva pancakes...

And off we go to walk a circuit encompassing all the stairs I could find around **Casa Loma**. There are hundreds of them!

Spadina Road

Walking northbound on Spadina Rd, you will reach the **Baldwin Steps** in 4 minutes. They are named after Dr. Baldwin who built the first house on the site in 1818.

3 From the top of the 110 steps, you will be rewarded by a view of Spadina Rd spreading down below, like a little Avenue des Champs-Élysées.

Initially built in wooden blocks, it has known many incarnations but the latest has reproduced the original zigzag pattern.

4 Upstairs, you'll get a glimpse of the castle to your left and **Spadina House** on your right. James Austin (founder of the Dominion

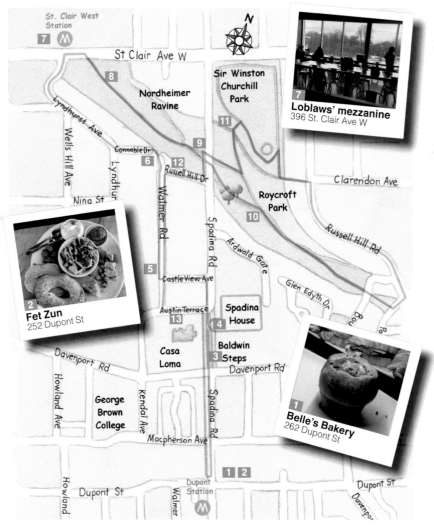

Loblaws' mezzanine
396 St. Clair Ave W

Fet Zun
252 Dupont St

Belle's Bakery
262 Dupont St

Bank, acquired the estate in 1886. His grand-daughter, who lived there until 1982, donated the house fully furnished to the City of Toronto. It opened as a museum in 1984. You can admire its gorgeous gardens and grounds for free.

Walmer Street

5 Walk up Spadina Rd then turn left on Castle View Ave. At the end of the street is the red facade of **Casa Loma**'s coach house on Walmer Rd.

6 At the end of Walmer Rd, you will access a cute little nook to your left, leading to Connable Dr, a quiet street meeting Lyndhurst Ave where we can see a series of chic townhouses with what seems like their own private little street.

Keep walking to St. Clair Ave W. **Loblaws**, across the street, houses various take-out options and a **Starbucks** counter. Its mezzanine is lined with bay windows and offers a pretty view of the trees in **Nordheimer Ravine** (polaroid #7 on map).

Nordheimer Ravine

You access the ravine from a staircase at the lights across from **Loblaws**.

8 **Nordheimer Ravine** includes a lovely gravel trail and a few dirt side trails. Don't worry, you can't get lost!

9 Walk until you are under the Spadina Rd viaduct, near the new popular dogs park. At this point you could climb up the staircase back to **Casa Loma** if you're short of time.

Otherwise, push on to **Roycroft Park Lands**.

Roycroft Park

10 Keep following the path into **Roycroft Park** (don't go up the hill to your left). The bucolic sinuous trail will lead you into **Glen Edyth Wetland**.

You can sometimes see volunteer gardeners clearing the bush. They've done a great job at rejuvenating the area. Now and then, you can see the backyards of some serious properties (always a bonus, isn't it?).

At the end of the park, keep walking up little **Poplar Plains Parkette**, turn left then left again on Russel Hill Rd.

Russell Hill Road

This beautiful road goes all the way up to St. Clair Ave W. It is especially charming at Clarendon Ave, with a stone wall on one side and a picture-perfect cottage-like house by the path on your left, where you will turn.

Sir Winston Churchill

The fork to your right will take you to the new staircase leading to the main plateau of **Sir Winston Churchill Park**.

11 You're standing on the **St. Clair Reservoir**, accounting for 10% of the entire city's water storage capacity. Follow the path to the small Art Deco house and go down the staircase to admire its big sister, both recently embellished with golden doors and trim.

Note that there is no winter maintenance for the stairs and trails. If the access to the stairs by the limestone house is blocked, you will need to take another longer path around it.

Either way, walk down towards the viaduct and climb up the stone steps under the bridge to Spadina Rd.

12 To your right is the lovely Russel Hill Dr. Hard to believe we're in Toronto, isn't it? The tiny road is wide enough to let one car go at a time and runs under an arch of greenery.

Casa Loma

13 Stroll southbound on Walmer Rd to Austin Terrace, home to the impressive **Casa Loma**.

It is Canada's largest house, with 98 rooms, which owner Sir Henry Pellatt had to let go in 1924, due to a financial hardship following WW1.

The **Terrace Grill** is a lovely patio in the back of the castle, offering an amazing view of the **Casa Loma** and access to the surrounding gardens. But it is only for the patrons who paid the admission fee and open May to August. I like to save this for when I have visitors from out of town.

Then, it's the last staircase back to your starting point down the **Baldwin Steps**, to Dupont St.

Now is a good time to mention that funky **Fet Zun** (252 Dupont St) has a vast patio which would be a great finale to this energetic walk.

NATHALIE'S **TIPS TO PLAN** THIS STROLL

For a shorter walk
If you're game for some stair climbing but not for the whole circuit, I recommend the following 2.6-km loop (40-min walk). Do #1 to #5 (the **Baldwin Steps** are not to be missed), then turn right at Russell Hill Dr (see #12) and take the stairs down to have a peak into the ravine (see #9). Then go back up and retrace your steps to #13, and back to **Casa Loma** and **Spadina House**.

About timing and logistics
• This is a lovely walk in the fall, with all the mature trees lining streets and the deep ravine. Beware, stairs and trails are not maintained in wintertime. They can get icy.

Romantic mood
• I still haven't had a chance to visit the elegant **Flor de Sal Restaurant**, located 100 metres east of the **Baldwin Steps** at 501 Davenport Rd. With its gorgeous decor and rave reviews, it would be the perfect romantic rendez-vous, if you are ready to splurge. We're talking fine dining with white linens, candlelight and quality service. The restaurant is divided into several dining rooms. I'd go for the Garden Room with access to a small patio in summertime. They also do lunch, which would be a bit more affordable. See the splendid photos on **www.flordesalrestaurant.ca**.

Family fun
• **Casa Loma** is quite impressive from the outside. Inside, young adventurers will appreciate the long tunnel leading to the stables, the visit to the tower, and the secret stairs in Sir Pellet's office. You will appreciate the richly decorated rooms and the access to the patio and gardens. See **www.casaloma.ca** for details and admission fees; see **www.escapecasaloma.com** to learn about their exciting **Casa Loma Escape Series**, with costumed actors and immersive sets.
• **Spadina House** (the full name actually is **Spadina Museum: Historic House and Gardens**) is a more intimate exploration of a three-storey large house built in 1866, immersing ourselves in the life of the rich Austin family during the 1900-1930 period. Visit **www.toronto.ca** and search *Spadina Museum*.

A little extra in the area
• Check the mini-walks #25 and #26 on page 230 in the last chapter **#torontourbangems**.

FOREST HILL
BELTLINE STROLL
17

For long conversations

You can walk and talk and get deep into conversation with your companion without fear of getting lost along this straight-line stroll. The **Beltline Trail** is Toronto's longest and narrowest park (so narrow in fact, that you won't see it on a regular map). Trees lining it on both sides form arches over our heads on many parts of the trail, making it the best fall outing for walkers. Running through posh neighbourhoods, it once was a train track built by private interest to solve commuter transportation problems in the 1890's. When you're ready to get back to civilization, there's a lovely stretch of Eglinton West to explore.

STROLL
17

Toronto area
MIDTOWN

Neighbourhood
Forest Hill
+ Chaplin Estates

Full loop
9.7 km (14,925 steps)

Time estimate
2 hr 25 min

Mindset
When you need a straightforward walk to avoid the crowds and foster great conversations... or better listen to your inner voice.

Subway & TTC
• Exit at **Eglinton West Subway Station** and take a 5-min walk eastbound to #1 (or exit at **Davisville Subway Station** and start the loop at **Oriole Park**).

Best parking
• Go on **Best Parking app** (www.bestparking.com) and search **1116 Eglinton Avenue West**.

Nathalie's TIPS
• See p. 143 for more tips to help you plan this walk.

First things first

1 The French bakery **Thobors** is only a 5-min walk from **Eglinton West Subway Station**, which makes it the perfect start for this walk. I love their croissants and pinwheels. (Did you know these pastries are called "viennoiseries"?).

It's also the perfect last stop up on your way home to stock up on amazing pastries for your loved ones.

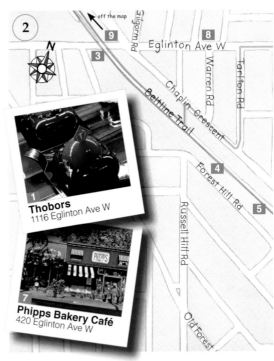

Thobors
1116 Eglinton Ave W

Phipps Bakery Café
420 Eglinton Ave W

Elm Ridge Dr
Beltline Trail
Allen Rd
Glenarden Rd
Old Park Rd
Ridge Hill Dr
Old Forest Hill Rd
Wembley Rd
Bathurst St
Shallmar Blvd
Chaplin Crescent
Eglinton West Station
Eglinton Ave W

START

Burnaby Blvd
Knoll Rd
Eglinton Ave W
Duncannon Dr
Elmsthorpe Ave
Braemar Ave
Highbourne Rd
Avenue Rd
Oriole Pkwy
Eastbourne Ave
Lascelles Blvd

Hotel Gelato
532 Eglinton Ave W

Beltline Trail
Urroff St
Forest Hill Road Park
Chaplin Crescent
Imperial St
Davisville Station
Dunvegan Rd
Forest Hill Rd
Avenue Rd
Oxton Ave
Oriole Park
Killbarry Rd
Lascelles
Yonge St

2 Walk eastbound on Eglinton Ave W and turn left on Bathurst St. You will access the **Beltline Trail** right after Shallmar Blvd, on the east side of Bathurst St.

The Beltline Trail

The **Beltline Trail**, wide and lined with trees all along, is heaven for joggers, bikers and walkers. In winter, without the bikes and speedy people, it gets much quieter.

Most of the **Beltline** runs through backyards of single houses. It is part of a private railway line completed in 1892 (which closed its passenger service only two years later due to the depression in the 1890's).

The City of Toronto bought part of the abandoned railway in 1972 to make a park, thanks to the work of City Councillor Kay Gardner, which explains why the 4.4 km section between Allen Rd and Mt Pleasant Rd is called the **Kay Gardner Beltline Trail.**

Eglinton murals

3 From Bathurst St, it's a 10-min walk to the Eglinton bridge running over the trail. Lovely murals on the walls feature detailed scenes blending nicely with their surroundings.

There used to be stairs taking us up to Eglinton but they are now gone, due to the Metrolinx construction nearby.

Larratt Parkette

4 Beyond the small **Larratt Parkette**, further

east, the trees are more imposing and you get a glimpse of the backyards of impressive properties (especially in the winter when the leaves are gone).

5 It's interesting to see how some chose not to connect to the trail while others built ambitious footbridges to enjoy their walks.

6 Past Avenue Rd, you'll reach the pedestrian bridge running over Yonge St. On the east side of Yonge is a staircase to get down to the street level.

You could take one of the two entrances to **Mount Pleasant Cemetery** and cross it to Moore Ave where the **Beltline** continues, on the other side of the street. But we won't.

Instead, walk north on Yonge St to Davisville Ave. Note that **The Bull: A Firkin Pub** along the way (1835 Yonge St) is a cool pub with London vibe open 11:30 am to 2 am, including booths and a pool table.

Oriole Park

Cross at Davisville Ave and walk into Chaplin Crescent, past **Davisville Subway Station**, until you reach a path on your left (facing Colin Ave). Take it to reach the big **Oriole Park**, which you will cross to get to Lascelles Blvd, back to the **Beltline**.

Turn right on the trail and walk until you get to the **Larratt Parkette**. Take the path on your right to Chaplin Crescent. Turn left, then right on Duncannon Dr, towards Eglinton Ave W.

Eglinton Avenue

If you still have the energy, the .5-km stretch between Duncannon Dr and Avenue Rd is full of great shops selling clothing, fashion or home accessories.

7 Check **Phipps Bakery Café** as you walk back to Castle Knock Rd. Their mural and mosaic in the back of the shop is truly cheerful. (Their mac & cheese and soup of the day are perfect after a stroll during the fall.)

8 If you are in no hurry, try **Hotel Gelato**, further west (532 Eglinton Ave W). This glam café is licensed and serves great breakfasts, treats, lunch and dinner with a charming attention to detail.

If you just want to grab coffee and a muffin, there's hip **Mad Bean** across the street (519 Eglinton Ave W).

Take nearby Tarlton Rd down to see a few very modern houses. Then turn right on Chaplin Crescent and look for the tiny **Robert Bateman Parkette** on your left (facing Russell Hill Rd). It's your way back to the **Beltline Trail**.

9 Right after Bathurst St, you will feel sheltered by the trees, which create a pleasing natural tunnel.

10 You'll pass the **Nicol MacNicol Parkette** before reaching the western end of the trail, at Allen Rd. (FYI: **York Beltline Trail** continues over 2.5 km further west, off Elm Ridge Dr.)

To return to Eglinton West Station, take the path on your left. Then turn left on Wembley Rd and right on Glenarden Rd.

NATHALIE'S **TIPS TO PLAN** THIS STROLL

For a shorter walk

If you don't have much time, or stamina, I suggest a 2.6-km loop (40-min walk) including **Phipps Bakery Café** (see #2). Go down Duncannon Dr to the **Beltline Trail** and turn right to reach the murals under the Eglinton bridge (see #3). Then, retrace your steps to go back to your starting point.

About timing and logistics

• The **Kay Gardner Beltline Trail** continues on the west side of Allen Rd, where its name changes to **York Beltline Trail**. You can access it by turning right when you reach the wall at Allen Rd, then turn left at Elm Ridge Dr. You'll see a paved path to your left right after you've crossed over Allen Rd. The trail then runs for 2.5 km, and ends a bit after Caledonia Rd.

• The **Kay Gardner Beltline Trail** also continues east of Yonge over .8 km to Mount Pleasant Rd, where you can go down stairs to cross **Mount Pleasant Cemetery** (more about this cemetery on page 120).

• The trail resumes at Moore Ave, across from the cemetery. It is now simply called the **Beltline Trail** and runs for an additional 2.5 km until it turns perpendicular to Bayview Ave and reaches a fork, past **Evergreen Brick Works** (more about this attraction on page 104).

Romantic mood

• If you are the sporty type, you might think it romantic to make it a challenge to walk the whole **Beltine Trail** together. You could make a day trip of it, taking the subway to **Eglinton West Station** and starting with croissants at **Thobors** (see #1), then doing the western part of the trail (read tips in the section above). Then you would do the 3.6 km walk east of Allen Rd to Yonge St. Further east, you'd walk .8 km and go downstairs to **Mount Pleasant Cemetery** to walk to the exit on Moore Ave, .5 km further. The end of the trail is 2.5 km away (read tips in the section above). You would then retrace your steps to Yonge St. Altogether, it's over 16 km. Note that **The Bull: A Firkin Pub** (1835 Yonge St, opening at 11:30 am till late at night) would be a well deserved stop. It includes booths, a pool table and a cool London vibe.

Family fun

• **Oriole Park** (see page 141) includes the lovely wheelchair accessible **Neshama Playground**, with a cute splash pad amidst mature trees.

• Nobody gets lost along the **Beltline Trail,** so one less stress! But the trail is cut by major streets west of Yonge St so... one more stress. Make sure your kids wait for you at the pedestrian crossways.

A little extra in the area

• Check the mini-walk #21 on page 228 in the last chapter **#torontourbangems**.

WEST TORONTO
RAILPATH STROLL
18

Art all around the block

One casually strolls around a neighbourhood, walks around the corner, and BAM!
You're hit by the colourful sight of a huge
mural splashed all over an unassuming wall.
The **Junction Triangle** area hosts some of
the best clusters in town for such surprises.
Not to be confused with **The Junction**, sitting along Dundas West, west of Keele, the
Junction Triangle is formed by the junction
of three railways, through Dupont, Bloor and
Dundas. This up and coming neighbourhood now hosts the **Ubisoft** company and
includes the **Museum of Contemporary Art**
next to the trendy **Drake Commissary**.

STROLL
18

Toronto area
WEST END

Neighbourhood
Junction Triangle

Full loop
7 km (10,770 steps)

Time estimate
1 hr 45 min

Mindset
When you are curious and want to feel the pulse of an emerging Toronto full of promises.

Subway & TTC
• Exit at **Dundas West Subway Station** and take a 2-min walk northbound (or exit at **Lansdowne Subway Station** and start the loop at #11).

Best parking
• There's free street parking along Wallace Ave and nearby streets.
• Go on **Best Parking app** (www.bestparking.com) and search **Drake Commissary Toronto**.

Nathalie's TIPS
• See p. 151 for more tips to help you plan this walk.

First things first
Two cool options to start this walk are located on Dundas St W, near the subway station.

1 **The Merseyside** is the closest to the station. It bakes some of the best scones in town, and makes great breakfast sandwiches and grilled cheese.

2 Further north, **Hula Girl Espresso Boutique** (see #2 on the map) has lots of attitude with its exotic mural on the facade and fun decor inside. They serve great lattes in a chill ambience.

It is a stone's throw away from the **Wallace Pedestrian Bridge** that will get you to the **West Toronto Railpath**, on the other side of the train track.

About the railpath
The **West Toronto Railpath** is one of the few rail-to-track projects in town.

3 The 2-km urban path was built in 2009 along railway rights-of-way established many years ago, that have been narrowed. A Phase 2 in the plans would continue from Dundas W to Liberty Village... but don't hold your breath.

From the bridge, the railpath runs up to Cariboo Ave, .8 km further north.

4 You won't miss the gorgeous fish mural on the back of the **Osler Fish Warehouse**, past Dupont St.

5 It is followed by a small hill offering a surprising country feeling to this part of town.

At Cariboo Ave return on the path to Dupont St.

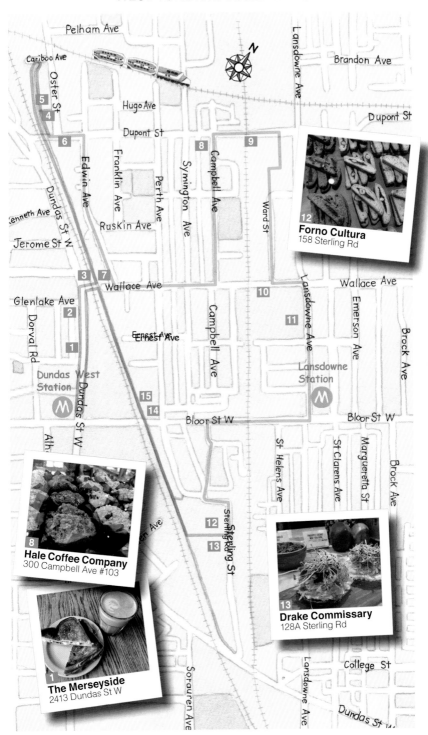

Forno Cultura
158 Sterling Rd

Hale Coffee Company
300 Campbell Ave #103

Drake Commissary
128A Sterling Rd

The Merseyside
2413 Dundas St W

If you look at the map, you will notice the two train tracks meeting on top of Cariboo Ave. It is one of the three points of what form the actual triangle giving its name to the neighbourhood. (The other points are below the compass rose on the map and south of Dundas St W.)

Dupont Street

6 Go down the stairs to street level to take in the long bike-themed mural under the viaduct on the south side (it was funded by the City's Graffiti Transformation Project).

The mural features a lineup of life-size cyclists riding towards a huge pile of retired tires. Impressive!

Edwin Avenue

Walk east on Dupont St to Edwin Ave, where you'll notice the funky flank of **Farmhouse Tavern** self-described as "a blackboard menu of farm driven food". (Not open for lunch but they have a brunch on weekends.)

After admiring the shiny roof of the **Ukrainian Orthodox Church of St. Andrew** across from the restaurant, walk southbound on Edwin Ave. Past Ruskin Ave, it becomes Sousa Mendes St.

7 You will transit from the older **Junction Triangle** to the up and coming modern section of this neighbourhood, where small shops are starting to pop up.

At Wallace Ave, turn left, then left again at Campbell Ave.

Campbell Avenue

8 As you walk north-bound on Campbell Ave, you will see the hip **Hale Coffee Company**.

Over the years, I have seen many cool places close in the area so I was wondering how such a big café could have survived. Then I found out that the equally hip company **Ubi-soft** opened an office near-by in 2010, with over 600 employees on the look-out for their caffeine fix.

9 Just east of Camp-bell Ave, on Dupont St, you'll come across Joel Richardson's captivating murals under the viaduct.

Knowing that the **Junction Triangle** is one of the few designated-for-employment areas left in Toronto adds context to appreciate these murals of men in suits.

Past the viaduct, right before Lansdowne Ave, take the pedestrian path to your right. It is a short-cut through the new condo development to reach Ward St. **Ubisoft** is the huge building at the corner of Ward St and Campbell Ave.

10 You'll find several cafés and restaurants around Wallace, including the funky **Café Neon** (241 Wallace Ave) near the pretty railway crossroad.

Lansdowne Ave.

There's a little Portuguese pocket at the corner of Wallace Ave and Lansdowne Ave. Despite the name, the **Paris Bakery** carries yummy Portuguese custard tarts. Then there's

Cantanhede O Bairradino's Portuguese chicken, the perfect stop for take-out (662 Lansdowne Ave).

11 Walking south, you'll see the lovely *Lansdowne Fence Streetscape* commissioned by the TTC to "temporarily" mask a sad-looking vacant lot. (Luckily, it's been there since 2010!) The intricate artwork by Marianne Lovink & Scott Eunson covers the fences on two sides.

Bloor Street West

Turn right on Bloor St W. It's seen better days. You can still see parts of the elegant series of delicate lace-like paintings under the graffiti.

That part of Bloor needs the kind of love it got from the collective of artists who covered the walls of the viaduct under the **Bloor GO Station**, further west.

MOCA Toronto

12 Cross Bloor St W at Sterling Rd and walk southbound on the narrow street lined with small houses. It will take you to the industrial park now home to the **Museum of Contemporary Art (MOCA) Toronto**, and the beautiful **Forno Cultura** café.

13 **Drake Commissary**, next door, is gorgeous and it opens at 8:30 am

14 There's a passage by the restaurant to get back to the **West Toronto Railpath**.

15 Make sure to go down the stairs to admire all the murals around the **Bloor GO Station**!

NATHALIE'S **TIPS TO PLAN** THIS STROLL

For a shorter walk

Walking on the **West Toronto Railpath** between **MOCA** and Bloor St W (see #12 to #15) is a 2-km loop (a 30-min walk). It will allow you to enjoy the railpath, admire the amazing street art collective under the viaduct near **Bloor Go Station** (taking the stairs down to street level), and have coffee and a bite in the new cultural hub.

About timing and logistics

• **The Friends of West Toronto Railpath**, a volunteer group committed to expanding, protecting and improving the railpath, have put together the very informative website **www.railpath.ca**.

• Visit **www.moca.org** to find out about the current exhibitions at the **Museum of Contemporary Art** (see #12).

• For those who love treasure hunting in second-hand stores (guilty!), I have noticed one of Toronto's biggest **Value Village** at 1319 Bloor St W, one block west of Landsdowne.

Romantic mood

• The **Drake Commissary** decor is absolutely gorgeous! The food is delicious and there are plenty of options for sharing. They have very good cocktails too!

Family fun

• I suggest a game of *I Spy* under the viaduct at **Bloor Go Station** (see #15), asking the kids to spot the animals. Over 30 artists joined forces to adorn the former grey area along Bloor St W.

• There's a *Photoautomat* machine inside the **Drake Commissary**! How retro is that? The whole family can try to fit in the photo booth (a big part of the fun) to have their black and white photos taken. Then all wait impatiently for them to drop to see how bad (or good) they are.

• Floor 1 of **MOCA Toronto** is free to the public. That's where you will find the café by **Forno Cultura** and a cool gift shop. Otherwise, admission fee is $10/adults, $5/seniors and it's free under 18 years old. The museum provides bilingual *Family Guides* to **MOCA** exhibitions for young visitors and their families. You can pick up at the front desk.

A little extra in the area

• Check the mini-walk #31 on page 233 in the last chapter **#torontourbangems**.

HIGH PARK
WATERFOWL STROLL
19

Beautiful nature, year-round

On certain weekdays in the spring, when the Sakura trees are in full bloom in **High Park**, it feels like everyone has decided to play hooky. In summer, people sit and sip refreshments at the central patio after a leisurely stroll along **Grenadier Pond** to catch sight of swans and cranes. During the fall, dark branches contrasting against a flamboyant background are picture perfect. In wintertime, careful walkers reach the path by the unfrozen part of the pond for a chance to observe a large raft of ducks probing the water. Year-round and everyday, beauty abounds in this urban oasis.

STROLL
19

Toronto area
WEST END

Neighbourhood
High Park

Full loop
4.4 km (6,770 steps)

Time estimate
1 hr 25 min

Mindset
When you must reconnect with nature, because you've gone too long without.

Subway & TTC
• Exit at **High Park Subway Station** and take a 1-min walk westbound.

Best parking
• Go on **Best Parking app** (www.bestparking.com) and search **High Park, Toronto**.

Nathalie's TIPS
• See p. 159 for more tips to help you plan this walk.

First things first
1 A good way to start or end this stroll is with a delicious Mexican bite at **Aztec's Mine**, a 2-min walk from the platform of **High Park Subway Station**, in the dead end of Parkview Gardens (no collector booth). They open at 11 am (closed on Mondays) and serve coffee.

Wendigo Pond
2 Cross Bloor St W at the foot of Clendenan Ave and take the long staircase down to the lovely secluded Wendigo Way.

To admire the properties in this charming tiny nook in Toronto, take the first right then turn left on Ellis Park Rd. Pretty, isn't it?

3 Walk through the parkette with small playground on your left, across the bridge, and turn right to reach **Wendigo Pond**. This is where, last winter, I encountered over a hundred ducks!

4 A bit further, we can often spot swans resting there on lazy summer days.

5 Then the grass gets taller and the wetlands more interesting, with a view over the big houses across the pond.

6 After that, huge trees by the water offer a relaxing setting inviting to idleness.

Up the hill
When you reach the wide-open space (with a giant Maple Leaf landscape in the middle), take the middle path going up the hill. Look past the hedges to

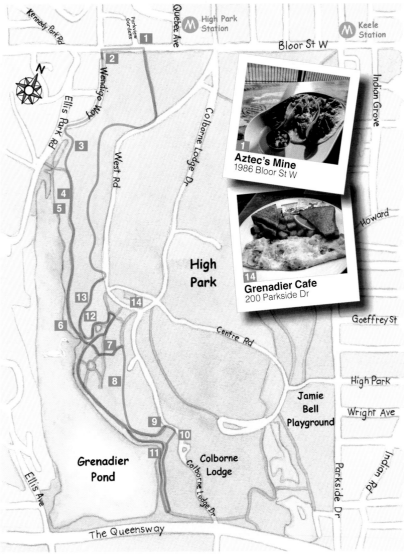

Aztec's Mine
1986 Bloor St W

Grenadier Cafe
200 Parkside Dr

see the intriguing symmetrical garden.

7 This is where you'll get the best view of the giant maple leaf and the sinuous paths.

8 Then turn right towards the grove. Last fall, this secluded section of the path was covered with a carpet of yellow Ginkgo leaves. It was truly magical!

9 Follow the path on your left when you exit the little forest and walk up towards Colborne Lodge Dr. Before you turn right on the street, you will pass bushes that turn pink in the fall. Lovely after the yellow explosion!

10 On Colborne Lodge Dr, you will soon see stairs on your right. Go down to return to **Grenadier Pond**.

Grenadier Pond

I think a stroll along **Grenadier Pond** is incomplete unless you've seen how gorgeous it is closer to The Queensway.

11 Turn left to stroll along the banks to see the weeping willows brush the water and the ducks mingling amidst the tall grass. Then return along the pond.

Hillside Gardens

Back to the hill with the giant Maple Leaf, take the first path to your left to walk up the gorgeous rockery within black iron fences.

12 The charming loop running around it all offers amazing views at every turn. **Hillside Gardens** includes two small bridges, little waterfalls and a pond giving Asian vibes.

The cherry lane

13 When you exit the rockery at the bottom of the hill, turn right into a lane going up. It is **High Park**'s famous cherry lane, absolutely spectacular from top to bottom when in full bloom (usually between mid-April to early May).

In other times, when it's not fighting with the cherry trees for your attention, you get to notice the sculpted face in a tree.

14 If you want to stop at the **Grenadier Cafe**, walk to the top of the cherry tree lane and go right on the street. The place opens at 7 am and offers a wide spread of breakfast, lunch and snack options. It includes a dining section and a large cafeteria with tables, plus a great outdoor patio.

Otherwise, when you get to the top of the lane, turn left on the road.

You have now three options to return to Bloor St W.

You may continue walking along the road. You will reach Bloor past the playground.

Or you may follow the first path you see on your left to return to the trail along the pond, back to the stairs.

Last time I visited, I chose to take the path running between the pond and the road. It is less frequented than other trails in the park and a bit more confusing but I liked the mature trees.

NATHALIE'S **TIPS TO PLAN** THIS STROLL

For a shorter walk

If you park at **Grenadier Cafe**, you can do a lovely 2-km loop (a 30-min walk) covering the gorgeous rockery, the cherry tree lane (see #12, #13 and #14) and the stroll along **Grenadier Pond** to **Wendigo Pond** (see #2 to #6).

About timing and logistics

• Note that **High Park Station**'s entrance with a collector booth is between High Park Ave and Quebec Ave. **Keele Station** is also staffed.

• The cherry on top of a Sunday (bad pun intended) at **High Park** is when you get to catch the Sakura trees in full bloom (see #13). Even on weekdays during the 7 to 10 days they are at their best (could be mid-April or early May), it feels like everyone has decided to play hooky, so you can imagine how crowded it can get on the weekends! Even parking can be a problem, despite all the parking lots in this huge park. Good thing **High Park Subway Station** is not too far! To find out the blossom status, go to **www.highpark toronto.com** then look for the *Cherry Blossoms/Sakura* tab.

Romantic mood

• Grab a picnic, bring cushions, and experience Shakespeare in High Park. It is Canada's longest-running outdoor theatre, presenting Shakespeare plays (what else?) with full decor, lighting and costumes in the middle of the park, Visit www.canadianstage.com to find out about their next summer production.

Family fun

• Follow a dirt path in the back of **Grenadier Cafe** to find the large labyrinth painted on a paved circle. You might want to quietly follow it and meditate... but the kids will use it as a race circuit!

• The small **High Park Zoo** was established in 1893 for deer, which is why the street on which it is located was named Deer Pen Rd, accessible east of **Grenadier Cafe**'s parking lot, a 2-min walk away. The zoo includes eleven paddocks with bison, llamas, peacocks, reindeer, highland cattle, wallabies, emus and sheep.

• A 4-min walk past the zoo, you will find one of Toronto's best playgrounds: the beautiful wooden castle of **Jamie Bell Adventure Playground**, filled with nooks.

• The park also includes a modern playground near a great splash pad closer to Bloor St W (off West Rd) as well as a large outdoor pool with slides (off Colborne Lodge Dr), and a trackless train in summertime.

A little extra in the area

• Check the mini-walks #31 and #32 on page 233 in the last chapter **#torontourbangems**.

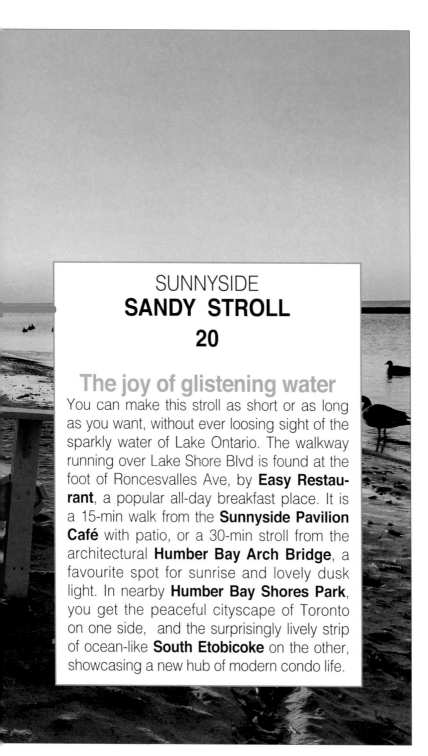

SUNNYSIDE
SANDY STROLL
20

The joy of glistening water

You can make this stroll as short or as long as you want, without ever loosing sight of the sparkly water of Lake Ontario. The walkway running over Lake Shore Blvd is found at the foot of Roncesvalles Ave, by **Easy Restaurant**, a popular all-day breakfast place. It is a 15-min walk from the **Sunnyside Pavilion Café** with patio, or a 30-min stroll from the architectural **Humber Bay Arch Bridge**, a favourite spot for sunrise and lovely dusk light. In nearby **Humber Bay Shores Park**, you get the peaceful cityscape of Toronto on one side, and the surprisingly lively strip of ocean-like **South Etobicoke** on the other, showcasing a new hub of modern condo life.

STROLL
20

Toronto area
WEST END

Neighbourhood
Roncesvalles + Humber Bay Shores

Full loop
6.4 km (9,845 steps)

Time estimate
1 hr 35 min

Mindset
When you are adamant you deserve a treat, such as the endless horizon and lapping waves of the lake... and a warm croissant!

Subway & TTC
• Streetcars **501** and **504**.

Best parking
• The best parking lot to enjoy this loop is just east of Ellis Avenue, by the beach.
• Go on **Best Parking app** (www.bestparking.com) and search **Sunnyside Pavilion Cafe**.

Nathalie's TIPS
• See p. 167 for more tips to help you plan this walk.

First things first
I've known **Cherry Bomb Coffee** for years, not realizing that they make the best chocolate croissants in town. When I showed up for coffee in the afternoon, their freshly made pastries were long gone.

1 Now that I've sampled a few of their treats, I am convinced the best way to start this stroll is early in the morning, a warm croissant in one hand and a coffee in the other. (Note that they have very limited seating.)

2 If you would rather sit for a full breakfast, you'll find the popular all-day breakfast **Easy Restaurant** at the intersection of Roncesvalles Ave and Queen St W.

On your way there, stop to check the mural in little **Grafton Avenue Park**. It depicts **Sunnyside Beach** back in the days when it was an amusement park.

At the foot of Roncesvalles Ave is the *Katyn Monument* in **Beaty Boulevard Park**, in memory of the thousands of Polish prisoners who died at Katyn forest during the invasion of Poland in WW2.

This is one of the many references to Eastern Europe one sees in this neighbourhood formerly known as Little Poland.

3 Walking on the fantastic pedestrian bridge crossing over the Gardiner will make you feel like you're leaving it all behind. First, there's the splash of colours by Justus Roe covering it all! Then, check out the view of the lake from this bridge!

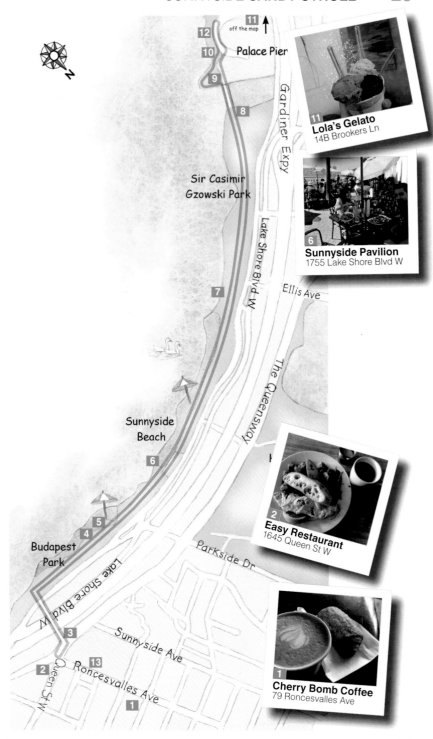

Palace Pier

Lola's Gelato
14B Brookers Ln

Sir Casimir
Gzowski Park

Sunnyside Pavilion
1755 Lake Shore Blvd W

Ellis Ave

The Queensway

Sunnyside
Beach

Easy Restaurant
1645 Queen St W

Budapest
Park

Lake Shore Blvd W

Parkside Dr

Sunnyside Ave

Roncesvalles Ave

Cherry Bomb Coffee
79 Roncesvalles Ave

Gardiner Expy

Lake Shore Blvd W

Sunnyside Beach

A few minutes west of the bridge, along the board-walk, is the cute **Sir Casimir Gzowski Playground**, with a wading pool in the shade of tall trees.

4 Note that the wading pool turns into a meditative labyrinth when summer is over.

5 This section of **Sunnyside Beach** is less frequented than the one around the **Pavilion**. There, I had the chance to witness a winter sunrise amidst ducks and seagulls.

Sunnyside Pavilion

6 Past the long **Gus Ryder Public Pool**, you'll reach the great water-front patio of seasonal **Sunnyside Pavilion**, a good place to observe swans while having lunch or a cocktail (it usually opens at 11:30 am). I haven't seen their courtyard in a while but it used to be lovely, with flowers and a classic fountain.

Don't miss the opportunity to admire the wonderful view from their second level if it is open.

7 As you walk westbound on the **Sunnyside Boardwalk**, you'll get closer to what looks like a second downtown. It is the new **South Etobicoke**. **Humber Bay Arch Bridge** is 1.3 km west of the restaurant.

Humber Bay Bridge

8 The deck of this award winning bridge is suspended under the twin arches by means of 44 stainless-steel hangers.

I spied carved turtles on its concrete foundation

9 On the other side, we can chill in Muskoka chairs peppered around the **Sheldon Lookout** while admiring Toronto.

10 The **Palace Pier**'s vast expanse of cobblestone is most inviting and the view is wonderful.

At dusk on a warm summer night, there are Fort Lauderdale vibes to the place! The locals living in the nearby luxury condos crowd the sidewalks and the bustling patios at **Eden Trattoria** and **Firkin on the Bay**, and guys in convertibles drive leisurely on Marine Parade Dr and Brookers Ln.

11 **Lola's Gelato** is a favourite stop for people of all ages.

12 The **Humber Bay Park E Trail** running through the waterfront park greatly contributes to the walkability of this neighbourhood.

Roncesvalles Ave

One thing to keep in mind when you return to Roncesvalles Ave, is that it's packed with little shops as cool as their promising names: **Knit Café**, **Jewel Envy**, **Coal Miner's Daughter**, **Scooter Girl Toys**, **Another Story Bookshop**, **Likely General**, **She Said Boom!**, **Scout**, **Fresh Collective**, to name a few. Add to this restaurants of all kinds, cafés, bakeries...

13 I personally love to browse inside the vintage store **Mrs. Huizenga** (28 Roncesvalles Ave).

NATHALIE'S **TIPS TO PLAN** THIS STROLL

For a shorter walk

The 2 km loop between **Easy Restaurant** and **Sunnyside Pavilion Café** (#2 to #6) offers the best of this stroll: the fun of overlooking the lake from the pedestrian bridge (wheelchair accessible) and a long walk on the beach (or on the wide paved path).

About timing and logistics

• The public washrooms in **Budapest Park**, beside the parking lot near the pedestrian bridge, is open year-round between 7 am and 6:30 pm, according to the City of Toronto's website.

• The temperature is often 5 degrees colder by the lake. Plan accordingly to fully enjoy your walk.

• Beware of black ice patches over the paved path in wintertime.

• When **Sunnyside - Gus Ryder Outdoor Pool** (located just east of **Sunnyside Pavilion**) was built in 1925, it was declared the biggest outdoor pool in the world! It is still Toronto's biggest outdoor pool, 91 metres long and 23 metres wide.

Romantic mood

• Want to watch a sunrise with your loved one? Check the sunrise schedule for the current time of the year and head east of #4. To enjoy the beautiful light of a sunset, go to the **Humber Bay Bridge** (see #8). It gets quite spectacular on a warm summer night.

• The retro **Revue Cinema** (400 Roncesvalles Ave, closer to Dundas St W and a 15-min walk from #1) is Toronto's oldest standing movie theatre. Over the years, the independent cinema has becomes a non-profit cultural community organization, the perfect spot for event-driven cinema, featuring original movie festivals as well as second-run programming The heritage site, built in 1912, underwent renovations in 2014 to restore its Edwardian and Art Deco charm. And it is surrounded by cool bars and restaurants to enjoy before or after your movie.

Family fun

• **Sir Casimir Gzowski Playground** is a lovely family spot offering simple pleasures in the shade (see #4). In summertime, the painted labyrinth turns into an original wading pool. Retro concrete dinosaurs chill nearby.

• Grab an ice cream cone at **Lola's Gelato** and enjoy it by the lake. Kids will have plenty of room to frolic on the grass while you admire the fantastic panorama.

A little extra in the area

• Check the mini-walks #30 on page 232, and #35 and #36 on page 235 in the last chapter **#torontourbangems**.

RUNNYMEDE
HILLY STROLL
21

Just the right mix

This stroll is part **Bloor West Village** (for some fun window shopping) and part **Swansea** (for a sneak into a lovely residential area). The mix of businesses on Bloor St W between Jane St and Runnymede Rd indicates a dynamic local life, with enough interesting stores, restaurants and patios to satisfy outsiders. Not to be missed, the prettiest **Shoppers Drug Mart**, built in the historic building which housed the Runnymede Theatre. The hilly roads in **Swansea** offer a unique panorama. You'll find a few staircases along the way to explore intriguing nooks and crannies.

STROLL
21

Toronto area
WEST END

Neighbourhood
Swansea

Full loop
4.2 km (6,460 steps)

Time estimate
1 hr 05 min

Mindset
When you want an intimate encounter with a neighbourhood that quietly goes along with its perfect life.

Subway & TTC
• Exit at **Jane Subway Station**.

Best parking
• Go on **Best Parking app** (www.bestparking.com) and search **Jane Subway Station**.

Nathalie's TIPS
• See p. 175 for more tips to help you plan this walk.

First things first

1 Can't think of a better way to start this walk than by enjoying a croissant with coffee on the second floor of **Ma Maison**, a genuine French bakery, which opened its second location in December 2019. "Ze" real thing! Plus, it's the perfect meeting point, two buildings away from **Jane Subway Station**.

Cross Bloor St W at Jane St. Walk eastbound on Bloor and turn right onto Armadale Ave.

Willard Gardens

Walk left on Mayfield Ave until you see the entrance to **Willard Gardens Parkette** (at the foot of Willard Ave).

2 Go down the stairs for a taste of **Swansea**'s unique topography of hilly terrain and winding roads, apparently similar to the topography found in Swansea, Wales, after which this neighbourhood is named.

3 In the elbow down the street, you'll find another staircase leading up a steep cliff to Yule Ave. Climb up and turn around to admire the view through mature trees.

Walk down Windermere Ave and turn right at Rambert Crescent. Where the street turns, you'll see a little clearing.

This is public space. Walk into it for a surprising panorama of the rooftops of the properties down below.

4 At Morningside Ave, turn right. This lovely country-like road runs towards S Kingsway.

Baka Gallery Café
2256 Bloor St W

Ma Maison
2432 Bloor St W

Janchenko's Bakery
2394 Bloor St W

Morningside Avenue

5 As you walk downhill, you'll have another great view and a peek at interesting properties.

6 Morningside Ave continues on the other side of S Kingsway, where it slowly climbs up a ravine.

7 The street ends at a staircase going up to Riverside Dr, along the black iron fence of a gorgeous house.

Riverside Drive

Walk left on Riverside Dr and take the first street on your right, Riverside Trail.

8 At the dead-end, you'll find stairs by a mansion. They lead down to another dead-end on the other side of Riverside Trail.

9 Once there, make sure to turn around to look at yet another lovely secluded nook in **Swansea**.

Brule Gardens

Turn right at Brule Gardens, once again so country-like with all the trees.

I suggest you walk up Brule Crescent and resume your stroll northbound on Brule Gardens. Keeping your right, you'll soon reach Bloor St W.

One & Two Old Mill

Walking eastbound on Bloor St W, look carefully across the street as you pass the imposing **Two Old Mill**. Can you see a curious dark figure by its entrance?

You will have to take a closer look! It is one component of *To the River*, the three-part concept by sculptor Alexander Moyle.

Each graceful bronze figure, covered in a black patina looks suspended in reeds in an invisible current. An apt theme, considering the **Humber River** is a 5-min walk away.

10 Walk to Riverview Garden and cross at the light to admire the beauty sleeping in the calm current of *Repose*. Nearby, the *Navigator* swims through the steady current with two followers. Both adorn the **One Old Mill** luxury condo.

11 You'll need to walk west to its sister **Two Old Mill** to take in the beautiful *Turbulence*, tossed by a tumultuous current. It is one of my favourite sculptures in Toronto. What a wonderful hidden gem!

Bloor Street West

The .7 km stretch on Bloor between **Jane** and **Runnymede Subway Stations** is packed with shops, restaurants and cafés.

12 I stocked up on Polish and Ukrainian pastries at **Janchenko's Bakery**. Tried a few things at nearby **Tzatz**. (I've noticed over a dozen fashion shops. It's an eclectic mix but you're bound to find one to your taste.)

13 Found a few cool gifts at lovely **Lemon & Lavender**.

14 Stopped at elegant **Baka Gallery Café** for coffee and a tasty bite.

15 For a big finish, visit... **Shoppers Drug Mart**! It used to be the Runnymede Movie Theatre, hence the unique architecture (which was preserved by the previous owner Chapters).

NATHALIE'S **TIPS TO PLAN** THIS STROLL

For a shorter walk

To get the feel of the neighbourhood, you could do a nice 2-km walk (30-min long) by walking from **Ma Maison** (see #1) and following #2 to #5. Then turn right at S. Kingsway, and right again onto Armadale Ave.

About timing and logistics

• There are many mature tress along this walk, which makes it a great one during the fall.

Romantic mood

• After the walk, you could get a fancy picnic and eat it in one of two nearby parks. It will be easier if you have a car but manageable on foot if you are in no hurry. For a European-style feast (think bread, pâté, cheese, fruit and pastries), there's the very well stocked **Cheese Boutique** (45 Ripley Ave), accessible from Ormskirk Ave, off S. Kingsway. It's a 12-min walk going south from Morningside Ave. **Étienne Brûlé Park** by **Humber River** is just 1 km away from **Ma Maison**. (Walk north on Old Mill Dr, between #10 and #11, and turn left on Catherine St.) **High Park** is also just 1 km away. If you turn east on Morningside Ave, it becomes Ellis Park Rd, with direct access to the park on your right. (See STROLL 19 on pages 152-159.)

Family fun

• With many hidden stairs and shortcuts at the end of dead-end streets, the walk between #1 and #9 will appeal to little adventurers. I would then suggest you return through the same route, and back to Bloor St W.

A little extra in the area

• Check the mini-walk #33 on page 234 in the last chapter **#torontourbangems**.

VILLAGE OF ISLINGTON
MURALS STROLL
22

Best mural spotting in town

The **Village of Islington BIA** convinced its members to commission the wonderful artist John Kuna (a graduate of **OCAD**, Toronto) to paint most of the gorgeous murals gracing many walls of what has become an outdoor gallery. This part of town includes access to **Mimico Creek**. It has not reached full gentrification yet, which adds to the fun of discovering these gems amidst little unpolished stores and unassuming restaurants, but cute businesses continue to pop up. You can eat macaroons at the **European Patisserie**, drink Turkish coffee at **Galata** and enjoy one more mural while eating inside Italian **Village Trattoria**.

STROLL
22

Toronto area
ETOBICOKE

Neighbourhood
Village of Islington

Full loop
4.6 km (7,075 steps)

Time estimate
1 hr 10 min

Mindset
When you want both culture and nature AND you are in no mood for concessions.

Subway & TTC
• Exit at **Islington Subway Station** and take a 5-min walk to **Tom Riley Park** (going north on Islington Ave and east on Aberfoyle Crescent).

Best parking
• Go on **Best Parking app** (www.bestpark-ing.com) and search **Village of Islington Murals**.

Nathalie's TIPS
• See p.183 for more tips to help you plan this walk.

Tom Riley Park
This walk starts with a babbling brook as **Mimico Creek** runs through the narrow **Tom Riley Park** (it ends in Lake Ontario, 5 km down the road).

1 Going north on Islington Ave from the subway station, turn right at Aberfoyle Crescent and look left for the park's entrance.

2 Chances are you will see ducks under the pedestrian bridge you'll encounter on your right. Once you're done watching them frolicking, return to the paved path and keep going north.

3 Pass under the bridge. Underpasses are always a great canvas for graffiti! Last time I was there, one of them read: "Tell your mother you love her."

4 Cross the next pedestrian bridge. On the other side, I found an access to the bank of the river with large boulders where I happily observed the heavy stream bubble over the rocks.

5 Up the path we see the back of the **Montgomery's Inn**, an 1840's era inn turned into a little museum. On Sundays, 1 to 4 pm, you can share a sweet and savoury combo plate and a pot of tea during their **Tea Time at the Inn**.

Islington Avenue
Now is the time to get your first glimpse of the gorgeous murals of artist John Kuna, commissioned by the local business community, turning this neighbourhood into an outdoor art exhibition.

Kipling

Renown Rd

Bloor St W

Dundas St W

9

10

Michael Power Pl

Royalavon

Avonhurst

Mabelle Ave

8

Islington
Seniors Centre

11

Village Trattoria
4901 Dundas St W

12

Cordova Ave

Burnhamthorpe Rd

12

7

Islington
Station
off the map

13

Burnhamthorpe Cres

Galata Cafe
5122 Dundas St W

9

1 2 3

Off the
map

Islington Ave

6

4

Dundas St W

5

Montgomery's Inn
4709 Dundas St W

5

Montgomery's
Inn
Montgomery Rd

Start the tour with a line-up of little clouds on a perfect shade of blue sky painted under the rail on the north/west corner of Dundas St W and Islington Ave.

In order to admire all the murals, it is better if you stick to one side of the road to the end, then return on the other side. I'll point out my favourites but know that there are 28!

6 The fact that we've just seen **Mimico Creek** makes *Aftermath* (4868 Dundas St W) even more impressive. It refers to Hurricane Hazel, October 14, 1954, when most land around the creek was flooded.

Burnhamthorpe Rd

7 The ambitious *Battersby's March* is easy to miss as it adorns the back wall of the **CIBC** (4914 Dundas St W). It features the three Canadian units that participated in the July 29th march in 1813 to secure Burlington against an imminent American threat.

A lovely rendering of bucolic **Mimico Creek** awaits at 4986 Dundas St W, facing a cute winter scene.

8 A bit further, I thought the mural on the west wall of 4994 Dundas St W showed a bomber dropping flyers to announce the end of WW2. Not at all! It illustrates a marketing stunt gone wrong when the wind blew hundreds of promo leaflets aimed at the school's football field during a game, across the nearby cabbage field...

Royalavon Crescent

The *Fishing in Mimico Creek* (5096 Dundas St W) is adorable.

9 So is *The Old Swimming Hole* (5126 Dundas St W), the last one on the north side. It is located near **Galata Cafe**, serving Turkish treats and dishes, and coffee in pretty cups.

Return to Royalavon Crescent to cross Dundas.

On the south side

10 John Kuna's latest (at the time of print) is a colourful and gorgeous mural with a bird theme (5101 Dundas St W).

Then, walking back eastbound on Dundas, it will be a few minutes before you encounter another mural. But make sure to look at **Village Paint and Wallpaper**'s window (4949 Dundas St W). It never disappoints!

11 My favourite mural sits at 4937 Dundas St W. Notice how the artist winks at painter Claude Monet's *Woman with Umbrella*?

12 At Cordova Ave, *The Faces of Islington* (4909 Dundas St W) cleverly illustrates the change from the predominately Eurocentric community in the 1950s into the diverse neighbourhood of today.

13 Further west, by the **Village Trattoria** (an inviting little Italian restaurant with its own indoor art), is the beautiful mural of a church (4901 Dundas St W).

The prettiest walk back to your starting point is through **Tom Riley Park** for one last peek at the creek.

NATHALIE'S **TIPS TO PLAN** THIS STROLL

For a shorter walk
The return loop along Dundas St W to see all the murals (see #6 to #12) is less than 2 km long, a 30-min walk, excluding the time to admire your favourites!

About timing and logistics
• The **Village of Islington** neighbourhood calls itself **Toronto's Village of Murals** and its **BIA** (Business Improvement Area) does everything in its power to reaffirm this well deserved status. On their website **www.village ofislington.com**, under the *MURALS* tab, you will find an interactive map indicating the location of the 28 murals. When you click on the red markers, a photo of the mural will pop. If you double-click that picture, you will get all the information on that specific mural.
• Stop at the **Village of Islington BIA**'s office (5048 Dundas St E) to get a free copy of the murals map.

Romantic mood
• Many of the murals are now lit at night, which makes for a lovely evening walk.

Family fun
• Historic **Montgomery's Inn** usually offers cool activities during the March Break.
• Children are well featured in John Kuna's paintings. Ask your kids to spot them in the murals. Little guys skating by the red fire brigade (4988 Dundas St E), tobogganing down the hill near **Montgomery's Inn** (5112 Dundas St E) and fishing in **Mimico Creek** (5096 Dundas St E) are truly charming.
• In *Fishing in Mimico Creek*, we can spy largemouth bass, rainbow trout, pumpkinseed sunfish, common shiner, white sucker and blacknose dace as well as the common snapping turtle, the leopard frog tadpole, the diving beetle, crayfish and a dragonfly nymph. (Try to find them all on the murals, and google them to find out if you're right.)

A little extra in the area
• Check the mini-walk #34 on page 234 in the last chapter **#torontourbangems**.

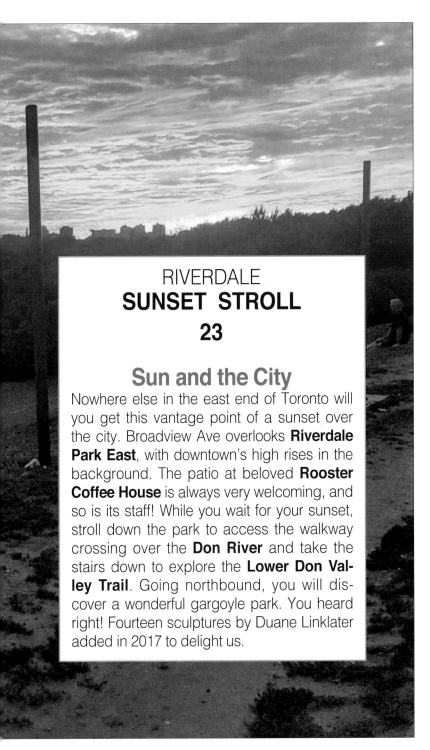

RIVERDALE
SUNSET STROLL
23

Sun and the City

Nowhere else in the east end of Toronto will you get this vantage point of a sunset over the city. Broadview Ave overlooks **Riverdale Park East**, with downtown's high rises in the background. The patio at beloved **Rooster Coffee House** is always very welcoming, and so is its staff! While you wait for your sunset, stroll down the park to access the walkway crossing over the **Don River** and take the stairs down to explore the **Lower Don Valley Trail**. Going northbound, you will discover a wonderful gargoyle park. You heard right! Fourteen sculptures by Duane Linklater added in 2017 to delight us.

STROLL 23

Toronto area
EAST END

Neighbourhood
Riverdale

Full loop
5.6 km (8,615 steps)

Time estimate
1 hr 25 min

Mindset
When you want to see Toronto through different lenses, from a wide-angle panorama to hidden treasure close-ups.

Subway & TTC
• Exit at **Broadview Subway Station**.
• Buses **504**, **505**, **506**.

Best parking
• •After 9 am, you might find room on Broadview along the park.
• Go on **Best Parking app** (www.bestparking.com) and search **Riverdale Park East**.

Nathalie's TIPS
• See p. 191 for more tips to help you plan this walk.

Sun and the city
I called this one the "sunset stroll" to get your attention to the fact that Broadview Ave offers one of the best viewpoints to fully enjoy the sunset over Toronto's cityscape.

If you have a chance, start it two hours before the sunset. (Read p.191 for tips on the best scenario to do so, depending on the sunset time of the year.)

But this walk is actually lovely at any time of day. If you decide to do it earlier in the day, I suggest you walk it in reverse, going southbound from the **Broadview Subway Station** straight to the **Rooster Coffee House**, then doing #10, #9, # 8, etc.

First things first
1 Use the Sunset Stroll as an excuse to have a drink or a bite in **Allen's** backyard patio! The food is fancier and a bit more expensive than one would assume in a pub but their backyard is unique. The daylight is gorgeous when filtered by the gigantic willow trees towering over the patio and at night, lights give them a dramatic look.

2 Then, walk west on Danforth Ave. Past the pizzeria and the ramp, you will find a passage leading to the ravine.

Riverdale Park East
3 You will walk over the ramp taking cars to the Don Valley Pkwy and go down stairs to join the dirt path running through a surprising forest of mature trees.

off the map

6

2

Danforth Ave

1

Broadview Station

Dearbourne Ave

Fairview Blvd

Broadview Ave

5

3

Hogarth Ave

Montcrest Blvd

Riverdale Pool

4

N

Don Valley Pkwy

Bayview Ave

Bain Ave

Broadview Ave

Riverdale Park East

Riverdale Park West

11

Langley A

7

Victor Ave

8

Gerrard St E

9

10

Allen's
143 Danforth Ave
1

11
Rooster Coffee House
479 Broadview Ave

11

10
Hanoi 3 Seasons
588 Gerrard St E

4 You can't go wrong. The trail leads to the bottom of the **Riverdale Park East**.

Keep walking along the soccer field and turn right to reach the pedestrian bridge and cross over the **Don River**.

5 Go down the stairs to your left to continue the walk going northbound on the **Lower Don River Trail**, which eventually gets quite luscious.

6 In 15 minutes, you will pass under the impressive **Prince Edward Viaduct** (linking Danforth Ave to Bloor St E) and have the pleasure to come across the most unexpected sight in such a setting: Duane Linklater's *Monsters for Beauty, Permanence and Individuality*.

The cast concrete sculptures are replicas of gargoyles and unusual sculptures on Toronto historic buildings.

I just love how the City is going about putting the **Don River Valley Park** on the map through this art program! (It is the natural space spanning from Pottery Rd to **Corktown Common**, including **Evergreen Brick Works**, and ongoing improvements in the last years are connecting it to and from surrounding neighbourhoods.

Bridgepoint Hospital

Return to the pedestrian bridge and back to **Riverdale Park East**. Then take the paved path to your right towards the hospital.

7 Go up the stairs to be amazed by the **Max Tanenbaum Sculpture**

Garden, overlooking the valley.

The colourful characters exude "joie de vivre". They are the work of Bill Lishman (better know as the man who inspired the Disney movie *Fly Away Home*) and his son Geordie, also a metal sculptor.

You can enter the modern hospital and take stairs down to its east entrance. Their courtyard is beautiful, with a reflecting pool.

8 Walk towards the street. On your left, you'll see the **Old Don Jail** turned into offices.

9 Cross Gerrard at the lights on your right and walk eastbound on the other side to reach the impressive traditional Chinese **Zhong Hua Men Archway**... in a 40-space parking lot.

10 If you still have one hour to kill before the sunset, I recommend drinks in funky **Farside** (which someone in a review aptly described as your grandma's basement circa 1970) or dinner at the small Vietnamese restaurant **Hanoi 3 Seasons** (see #10 on map).

Rooster Coffee House

11 It will take you 5 minutes to walk to the **Rooster Coffee House**. The place is so welcoming. There are pastries under glass bell jars, little trinkets to look at, a communal table, great coffee, and cool people behind the counter.

It takes approximately 15 minutes to walk back up to Danforth Ave while admiring the fantastic view over the park.

NATHALIE'S **TIPS TO PLAN** THIS STROLL

For a shorter walk

The main appeal of this walk is the beautiful cityscape you get when facing **Riverdale Park East**. For a lovely 2.5-km loop (40-min walk), I suggest you start at **Rooster Coffee House** (see #11), walk northbound on Broadview Ave to the northern end of the park at Montcrest Blvd and return. Reach the paved path going down at the southern end of the park, just around **St. Matthew's Lawn Bowling Clubhouse**. (This historic house used to be on Gerrard St, near the **Old Don Jail**. It was relocated in 2009!) Go check the **Don River** from the pedestrian bridge, then return to the park and take the path on your right to enjoy the lively characters on the west flank of **Bridgepoint Hospital** (see #7).

About timing and logistics

• Toronto's sunset times found on **www.timeanddate.com** are:
May 1st (8:20 pm), June 1st (8:50 pm), July 1st (9 pm), August 1st (8:40 pm), Sept. 1st (7:50 pm), and Oct. 1st (7 pm).
• It is quite interesting to learn more about the City's vision for what is now called the **Don River Valley Park**, encompassing **Evergreen Brick Works** but covering the whole green area from Pottery Rd to **Corktown Common**. Duane Linklater's *Monsters for Beauty, Permanence and Individuality* is part of their Don River Valley Park Art Program to put art in natural environment. Visit **www.donrivervalleypark.com**.

Romantic mood

• You can watch the sunset from the outdoor patio on the west side of **Bridgepoint Hospital**! Every time I have been there, there was outdoor furniture to sit on. It is accessible from the paved path at the bottom of the park, leading you to the multi-level patio/outdoor art gallery.
• **Allen's** backyard patio with huge willow trees is unique in Toronto.

Family fun

• There's a **Tim Hortons** on the main floor inside **Bridgepoint Hospital**. You could grab coffee and treats and take stairs to the second floor to access the outdoor patio to get a closer look at the fun characters. The patio has a multi-level design, perfect for young explorers.
• If you choose to take your kids to the gargoyles (see #6), I suggest you don't tell them what awaits around the corner. When they finally find the sculptures, allow them the pleasure of leading you to their discovery. (Try to resist the temptation to tell them you knew about it! Don't spoil the fun! You can tell them in 20 years.)

A little extra in the area

• Check the mini-walks #39, #40 and #41 on pages 237-238 in the last chapter **#torontourbangems**.

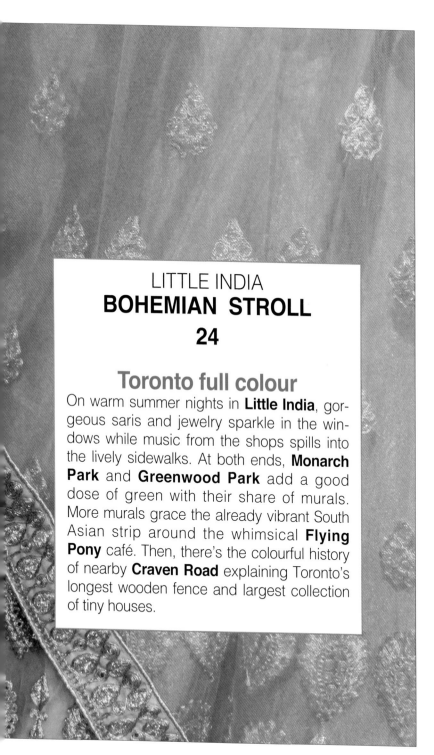

LITTLE INDIA
BOHEMIAN STROLL
24

Toronto full colour

On warm summer nights in **Little India**, gorgeous saris and jewelry sparkle in the windows while music from the shops spills into the lively sidewalks. At both ends, **Monarch Park** and **Greenwood Park** add a good dose of green with their share of murals. More murals grace the already vibrant South Asian strip around the whimsical **Flying Pony** café. Then, there's the colourful history of nearby **Craven Road** explaining Toronto's longest wooden fence and largest collection of tiny houses.

STROLL
24

Toronto Area
EAST END

Neighbourhood
The Danforth
+ Little India

Full loop
6 km (9,230 steps)

Time estimate
1 hr 30 min

Mindset
When you need to add colour and whimsy to your day.

Subway & TTC
• Exit at **Coxwell Subway Station** (or at **Greenwood Subway Station**).

Best parking
• Plenty of free street parking in dead-end streets south of **Monarch Park**, with a small path leading to its southern entrance.
• Go on **Best Parking app** (www.bestparking.com) and search **Coxwell Subway Station**.

Nathalie's TIPS
• See p. 199 for more tips to help you plan this walk.

Coxwell Station

1 A good way to start this colourful walk is by admiring the *Coxwell Laneway Mosaic Mural* on the 70-metre yellow wall framing two sides of the **Coxwell Subway Station**, from the exit, on the left side, to the **Green P** parking lot on Danforth Ave.

This community project led by Cristina Delago for **East End Art** was created in 2016.

First things first

2 You can stop for coffee and croissants (or much more decadent treats) at **Pâtisserie La Cigogne**, a bit further east. They open at 7:30 am on weekdays and 8 am on weekends.

Then walk southbound on Craven Rd. As you walk along this narrow street, you'll notice that the houses on the left are facing the backyard of their neighbours.

It turns out there's a good reason for that, which will become more obvious when you reach Craven Rd on the other side of **Monarch Park**.

Monarch Park

3 Turn right on Hanson St, which becomes Felstead Ave, and take the path into the park (at the foot of Monarch Park Ave). **Monarch Park** is a vast park with mature trees, especially beautiful in the fall.

4 Follow the path past the public skating rink. nicely adorned with a long yellow dragon. You will reach a tunnel lively with

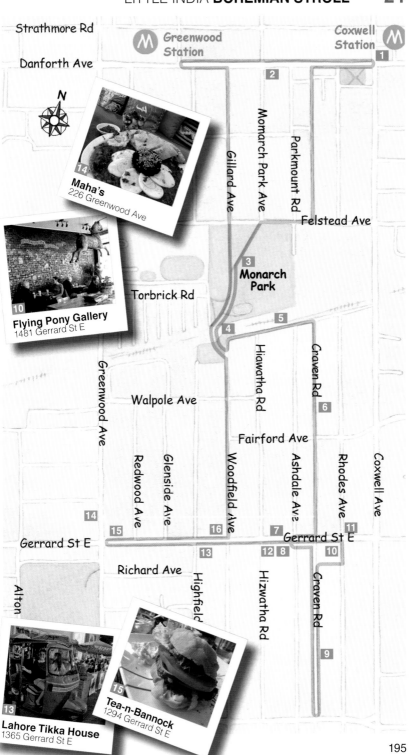

Strathmore Rd

Danforth Ave

Greenwood Station

Coxwell Station

1

2

N

Gillard Ave

Momarch Park Ave

Parkmount Rd

Felstead Ave

14
Maha's
226 Greenwood Ave

3
Monarch Park

Torbrick Rd

10
Flying Pony Gallery
1481 Gerrard St E

4 **5**

Hiawatha Rd

Craven Rd

Walpole Ave

Greenwood Ave

6

Fairford Ave

Redwood Ave

Glenside Ave

Woodfield Ave

Ashdale Ave

Rhodes Ave

Coxwell Ave

14

15

16

7

11

Gerrard St E

Gerrard St E

13

12 **8**

10

Richard Ave

Highfield

Hizwatha Rd

Craven Rd

Alton

13

15
Tea-n-Bannock
1294 Gerrard St E

9

13
Lahore Tikka House
1365 Gerrard St E

street artist Elicser's recognizable characters.

5 On the other side, look carefully into the dead end to see the narrow path linking all the dead-end streets south of the train track. Follow it until you reach Craven Rd.

Craven Rd

Craven Rd is unique (some call it **Tiny Town**)! It features the largest collection of tiny houses (500 sq ft).

In the 1890's, tiny lots were sold on its east side, outside the limits of Toronto. It means that the taxes were low and there were no services. A "shack town" emerged, allowing poor working families to own land.

The City eventually widened the lane, expropriating part of Ashdale Ave's lots on the west side.

6 A deal was made to put up Toronto's longest wooden fence to prevent the shack owners from trespassing.

7 Back to the walk. Go southbound on Craven, turn right on Gerrard St E and cross at Ashdale Ave.

8 This is my favourite intersection, with a cute mural facing the colourful **Chandan Fashion** store selling everything from simple clothes to special occasion attire. (The wedding dresses are spectacular.)

Walk eastbound on Gerrard St E and turn right at Craven Rd.

9 We can still see a few 500-sq-ft houses but most have expanded over the years. Some have added a second floor, an extension in the back, or both.

Around 241 Craven Rd, you will see a funky outdoor art installation. Some artists have also used the wooden fence as an outdoor art gallery.

I suggest you walk to Dundas St E and return to Gerrard St E, but Craven Rd has more tiny houses south of Dundas down to Queen St E.

Gerrard Street

10 Turn right on the lane before Gerrard St E, where colourful murals set the tone for the extreme whimsy of the **Flying Pony Gallery** around the corner. They bake great snacks, and the owner/painter has created a hilarious mural inside.

11 Nearby New Age **Hamsa Heaven** is in the same spirit. Also noticeable eastbound on Gerrard: **Blue Crow Gallery**'s gift ideas, wholesome meals at **Lazy Daisy's Café** and decadent donuts at **Glory Hole**.

12 One truly exotic stop going west on Gerrard St E is the **Maharani Emporium**.

13 There's ambience in **Lahore Tikka House**, lined with fabrics inside, with rickshaws at the door.

14 Can't be in this part of town without mentioning **Maha's** welcoming restaurant serving homemade Egyptian food.

15 And what about **Tean-Bannock**, the small Indigenous place where one can eat a delicious bison burger served in fried bannock bread!

16 From Gerrard St E, turn left on Woodfield Ave to return to your starting point.

NATHALIE'S **TIPS TO PLAN** THIS STROLL

For a shorter walk
The following 1.5 km loop (a 25-min walk) includes the intriguing Craven Rd and the most whimsical café in **Little India**. Start at the **Flying Pony Café** (see photos #10 and #11), then turn left on Craven Rd to enjoy #9. Return to Gerrard St E and turn left. Walk westbound to see #7, #8 and #12, then go north at Hiawatha Rd to Fairford Ave. Turn right then right again at Craven Rd, to see more of the tiny houses.

About timing and logistics
• The colourful windows on Gerrard St E look even better when brightly lit on a warm summer night.
• One can make amazing curtains with the pieces of fabric sold to make saris in several shops on Gerrard St E. They usually are 6 yards long or more, and include a pretty border. You can find lovely ones for $25. Imagine what you can get for $50!

Romantic mood
• Share a bit of history with your partner before heading to Craven Rd. A good resource to learn more about this unique street is **www.leslieville history.com/craven-rd-fence**, **www.leslievillehistory.com/erie-terrace-to-craven-road** and **www.leslievillehistory.com/craven-road**.
• **Sauce on Danforth** (1376 Danforth Ave) is a great cocktail place in a very cool decor, with a bit of a French boudoir meets Goth vibe to it.

Family fun
• Many of the shops exhibiting colourful affordable shirts on the sidewalk sell inexpensive shiny trinkets inside. Fun to explore with little treasure hunters.
• The annual 2-day **Festival of South Asia** (organized by the **Gerrard India Bazaar BIA** on a weekend in the middle of July) is quite fun for the whole family. Gerrard St usually turns carless for the occasion, from Glenside Ave to Coxwell Ave. Last time I attended, we saw a giant papier maché elephant, great dance troupes on a small stage, street merchants selling treats, all day and evening. Many South Asian visitors attended wearing their colourful traditional attire. Consult **www.festivalofsouthasia.com** for details.
• In winter, **Greenwood Park** includes a lovely pleasure-skating trail made of natural ice (weather permitting). At any time, you can see the statue of a little boy with his tiny toy car on a side bench. Google *Death of Jeffrey Baldwin*, to find out the touching story of this little boy.

A little extra in the area
• Check the mini-walk #46 on page 240 in the last chapter **#torontourbangems**.

THE BEACH
SOOTHING STROLL
25

Shades of green and blue

Stressed out by the compulsive busyness of your life? This nature stroll will do the trick! There's nothing more soothing than the serene shelter of a ravine or the noise of waves brushing the shore, and nothing so relaxing as the sight of sparkling water. Letting your eyes scan the endless horizon is like meditation. Rule of thumb, the further east you'll walk in **The Beach** neighbourhood (still The Beaches to many), the farther you'll get away from the crowd. This walk also includes a few dips into Queen St E to indulge with French pastries or yummy salty muffins. Also very soothing...

STROLL
25

Toronto area
EAST END

Neighbourhood
The Beach
+ Upper Beaches

Full loop
5.2 km (8,000 steps)

Time estimate
1 hr 20 min

Mindset
When you want
the relaxing feeling
of being in a coastal
town.

Subway & TTC
• Streetcar **501**.

Best parking
• There's plenty of
street parking on
MacLean Ave and
Pine Crescent. I also
like to park near the
ravine's entrance on
Glen Manor Dr E.
• The further east you
go, past **Kew Gardens**, the easier it is
to find free parking
spots on the streets
south of Queen Street.

Nathalie's TIPS
• See p. 207 for more
tips to help you plan
this walk.

First things first

1 Utterly charming
Tori's Bakeshop is
a great meeting point for
this stroll leading you first
to the ravine. They serve
very good vegan scones,
mini donuts, sandwiches
(non-dairy options only for
their coffee).

If you would rather
begin with a classic breakfast, go to **The Beacher
Cafe** (polaroid **#2** on map).

Glen Manor Drive

3 Walk westbound on
Queen St E to **Ivan
Forrest Gardens**, just east
of Glen Manor Dr, a unique
little park with lovely rockery
and fountain.

Then, take the right
fork where Glen Manor Dr
splits in two.

4 Take the time to
admire the park from
the pedestrian bridge you'll
find to your left (at the foot of
Pine Glen Rd).

Glen Stewart Ravine

5 Then walk up Glen
manor Dr E to **Glen
Stewart Ravine**'s entrance,
to your right. You will soon
see the beautifully designed
staircase, the sort of addition one would expect in a
national park! This is what
we get when talented urban
planners are given a $1 million budget to improve a
municipal ravine.

6 You will walk up and
down slopes under
mature trees. Here, it is easy
to forget we are in Canada's
biggest city! When you come
upon a fork, embark on the
path to your right. It will take
you up to Beech Ave through
a wilderness trail.

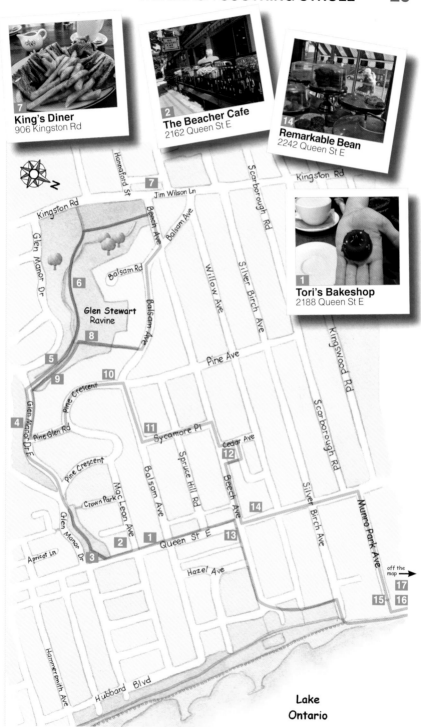

King's Diner
906 Kingston Rd

The Beacher Cafe
2162 Queen St E

Remarkable Bean
2242 Queen St E

Tori's Bakeshop
2188 Queen St E

Lake
Ontario

5

6

7

7 I've got a few favourite spots on Kingston Rd, turning right off Beech Ave. There's **King's Diner**, including a cute mezzanine at the back. The new owners have redecorated and offer a small menu of fresh options. They open from 8 am to 3 pm (closed on Mondays).

The Great Escape Book Store at 957 Kingston Rd, two blocks further east on the south side, has been around for over 50 years. With a charming small town feel, it carries mostly second-hand titles and has an outdoor reading patio and rose garden in the back.

Balsam Avenue

Walk southbound on Balsam Ave. Across from the schoolyard, you'll notice the fenced entrance to the ravine.

8 It will take you to the long stairs going down the ravine. This is where you'll get the best panoramic view over the ravine.

9 Turn left at the foot of the stairs. You will walk by a stream singing through pretty wetlands and reach Glen Manor Dr E where you'll turn left, seeing major properties along the way.

10 Turn left at Pine Glen Rd and left again into the steep and cobbled Pine Crescent. It will take you to a beautiful old house at the corner of Pine Crescent & Balsam Ave. Turn right.

11 Then turn left on lovely Sycamore Place.

12 Take Beech Ave to your right. Turn left into Cedar Ave and take the alleyway to your right.

Then, look for an odd public sidewalk crossing the backyards of the houses on Cedar Ave.

Back to Beech Ave, turn left to reach Queen St E, my favourite corner in the whole neighbourhood! Everything one needs to be happy is at a stone's throw from that intersection!

13 On your right, there's **Outrigger**'s lovely patio with a running fountain, and further, the artisanal gelato of **Ed's Real Scoop**. Across the street, **Chocolates by Wickerhead** offers some of Toronto's most creative artisanal chocolates.

14 On your left, is the **Fox Theatre**, my favourite independent cinema, near **Remarkable Bean** selling scrumptious savory muffins. And across the street awaits the **Garden Gate** with retro booths and outdoor patio.

Beach houses

15 Walk eastbound to Munro Park Ave, and turn right. Stairs at the end of the street will take you to the beach. Only locals seem to visit this segment of the beach.

16 Walk on the sand to your left to admire dreamy beach houses. Some of them have infinity pools! The life!

17 The 3-km boardwalk running along **Kew-Balmy** and **Woodbine Beaches** is just 100 metres to your right but for a big finish, I suggest you go to the end of the beach to see the Art Deco **RC Harris Water Treatment Plant** and admire its spectacular view.

NATHALIE'S **TIPS TO PLAN** THIS STROLL

For a shorter walk
The truly soothing section of this stroll is the 25-min loop between #14 and #16 and back to Beech Ave & Queen St E (with all the decadent places to treat yourself before or after the walk). It will allow you to admire the fantastic beach houses along the most quiet part of the beach, with the endless horizon.

About timing and logistics
• Rule of thumb: the further east you go, past **Kew Gardens**, the better your chances to find free street parking on the streets south of Queen St E. This stroll is half a km east of **Kew Gardens**, so parking shouldn't be a problem.
• Dogs really, really dig the off-leash dog park at the foot of Silver Birch Ave.

Romantic mood
• The **Great Escape Book Store** (see p. 204) has been producing an intimate live music concert series that seems utterly charming. It is held in their backyard garage! Check the *Sounds of the Summer* tab on their website **www.greatescapebookstore.com**. This bookstore has been over 50 years in this same spot!
• Get decadent treats at **Chocolates by Wickerhead** (see #13) or classic Belgian chocolates from **The Belgian Chocolate Shop** (2455 Queen St E, just before turning into Munroe Park Ave) and go to eat them by the beach.
• Check **Fox Cinema**'s listing (see #14) for a romantic movie, go for a walk before the presentation, and a drink on one of the nearby patios after (or vice versa).

Family fun
• The little and shallow creek near the entrance of **Glen Stewart Ravine** is an invitation to float small paper boats down the stream.
• **Ed's Real Scoop** (see p. 205) is a family favourite. This was the first outlet they opened, back in 2000. And in case you were wondering, the difference between ice cream and gelato is that ice cream is made with milk and cream, and gelato has much less fat but a little more sugar. Sorbets are vegan and dairy-free.
• The best place in town to roll down a grass hill is at **RC Harris Water Treatment Plant** (see #17). No contest.

A little extra in the area
• Check the mini-walk #47 on page 241 in the last chapter **#torontourbangems**.

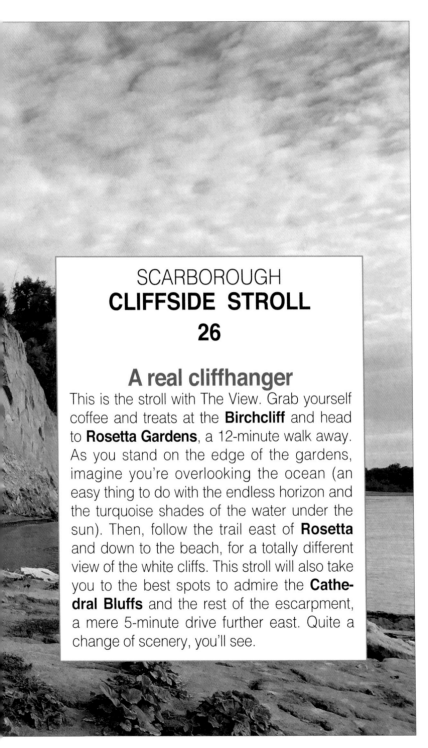

SCARBOROUGH
CLIFFSIDE STROLL
26

A real cliffhanger

This is the stroll with The View. Grab yourself coffee and treats at the **Birchcliff** and head to **Rosetta Gardens**, a 12-minute walk away. As you stand on the edge of the gardens, imagine you're overlooking the ocean (an easy thing to do with the endless horizon and the turquoise shades of the water under the sun). Then, follow the trail east of **Rosetta** and down to the beach, for a totally different view of the white cliffs. This stroll will also take you to the best spots to admire the **Cathedral Bluffs** and the rest of the escarpment, a mere 5-minute drive further east. Quite a change of scenery, you'll see.

STROLL
26

Toronto area
SCARBOROUGH

Neighbourhood
Cliffside
+ Birch Cliff

Full loop
6.4 km (9,845 steps)

Time estimate
1 hr 35 min

Mindset
When you want
to leave it all behind
and be in the beautiful
present moment.

Subway & TTC
• Bus **12**.

Best parking
• There's free parking
at **Rosetta McClain
Gardens**.
• There's free street
parking on Scarboro
Crescent and adjacent
streets around **Scar-
borough Bluffs Park**.
• There are paying
parking lots in **Bluff-
er's Park**.

Nathalie's TIPS
• See p. 215 for more
tips to help you plan
this walk.

First things first

1 I usually use this stroll
as an excuse to drive
through **The Beach** along
Queen St E and make a stop
at **Remarkable Bean** to
grab some of their amazing
salty muffins and a cup of
coffee.

**Rosetta McClain
Gardens** is a 12-min drive
further east, along Kingston Rd.

2 **The Birchcliff** would
also be a great meet-
ing point. This pretty café
serves great treats. It is a
10-min walk from **Rosetta
Gardens**.

3 You will notice that
the birch theme is
strong inside the café and
out on surrounding build-
ings in this neighbourhood
called **Birch Cliff**.

The Gardens

From Kingston Rd, you can
access **Rosetta McClain
Gardens**' parking lot, just
before Glen Everest Rd.
(The bus stops at Lakehu-
rst Dr, a 2-min walk away.)

4 You could easily tour
the gardens in 15 min-
utes but there's a lot to be
admired here. In the cen-
tre, there are symmetrical
raised planter beds around
a few large boulders.

5 The site is perched
atop the cliffs so you'll
be able to catch a breathtaking view of Lake Ontario, 60 metres below, as you
take a turn along the trail.
In the right conditions, the
water takes on a beautiful
turquoise hue.

6 In the eastern section,
you'll find a mature
and luscious forest (beautiful in the fall).

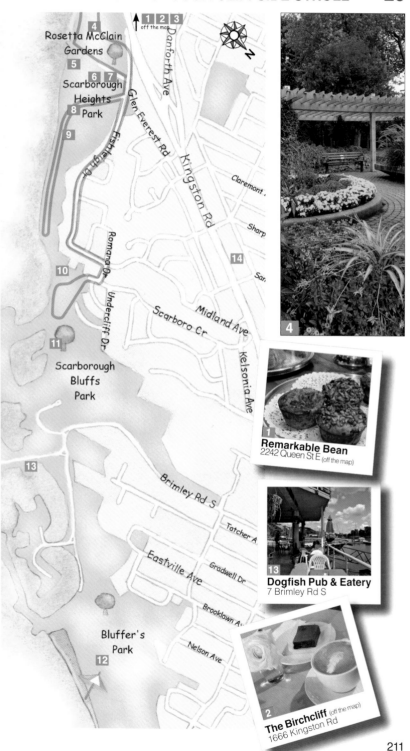

1 2 3 off the map

Rosetta McClain Gardens **4**

5

Scarborough Heights Park **6** **7**

8

9

Danforth Ave

Glen Everest Rd

Fishleigh Dr

Kingston Rd

Claremont

Sharp

14

Sar

10

Romana Dr

Undercliff Dr

Midland Ave

Scarboro Cr

Kelsonia Ave

11

Scarborough Bluffs Park

13

Brimley Rd S

Tatcher A.

Eastville Ave

Gradwell Dr

Brooklawn A.

Bluffer's Park

Nelson Ave

12

1 **Remarkable Bean**
2242 Queen St E (off the map)

13 **Dogfish Pub & Eatery**
7 Brimley Rd S

2 **The Birchcliff** (off the map)
1666 Kingston Rd

7 In the northeast corner of the park is an elegant vine-covered trellis near a rose garden.

Back towards the parking lot are romantic ruins of the old McClain house. Exit there and turn right on Glen Everest Rd.

8 Then take the closed road to your right (between the garden plots and Fishleigh Dr) to get down to the beach. Note that it is steep and can be slippery when wet.

Cathedral Bluffs

Huge boulders create break walls. Lovely tall grasses run up the hill.

9 In 10 minutes, you'll get a fantastic view of the white cliffs carved in such a way to have inspired the name the **Cathedral**. Positively surreal!

Want to see it from above? Back to Glen Everest Rd, follow Fishleigh Dr on your right. It turns left into Midland Ave. Take the first street right (Romana Dr), then turn right at Scarboro Crescent. You've arrived at **Scarborough Bluffs Park** (or **Cathedral Bluffs Park**).

Entering the park at the foot of Scarboro Crescent, walk towards the lake for the grand panoramic view over the white cliffs.

10 Looking to your right, you'll discover the **Bluffs**, covered with trees.

Looking down to your left, you'll see the 400 acres of **Bluffer's Park**, with its marina, meandering roads and more cliffs with rocky peaks.

Bluffer's Park

If you still have the energy, I strongly recommend you go east to visit **Bluffer's Park**, at the foot of Brimley Rd S. (I admit it's easier if you have a car.)

From Kingston Rd, it is 1.5 km to the trails on the **Cathedral**'s side, near the first parking lot.

11 The trails in that section of the park include a wetland section with boardwalks (I've seen otters!), four sytems for storm water treatment, and access to the small beach at the foot of the **Cathedral**.

The popular **Bluffer's Park Beach** spreads east of the last parking lot, 2.3 km away from Kingston Rd. Warning: come early on bright summer days. The parking lots fill quickly.

12 You reach the beach via a trail by the parking lot. When the sand is dry, it is some of the finest I've seen in the Greater Toronto Area.

The seasonal **Bluffer's Restaurant** is located at the foot of Brimley Rd in the marina. It includes **Dogfish Pub** (polaroid **#13** on map), offering lighter, more affordable fare, with a view. (Both open daily at least from 11 am, April to October.)

The Murals

On your way back, try to spot the ten murals to be found left and right between Warden and Midland (a **Mural Routes** initiative).

14 My favourites are the rowboat approaching the cliffs (2384 Kingston Rd) and the marching band (1577 Kingston Rd).

NATHALIE'S **TIPS TO PLAN** THIS STROLL

For a shorter walk
The paved path running around **Rosetta McClain Gardens** is roughly 1 km long, easily accessible from Rosetta's parking lot. Not only is it one of the prettiest gardens in Toronto, already a good reason in itself to visit this park, you will also get to enjoy the magnificent view of Lake Ontario from above. They have seasonal washrooms on the premises.

About timing and logistics
• Dogs are not allowed in **Rosetta McClain Gardens**, and locals will remind you in no uncertain terms if you show up with your pet.
• A major makeover was going on around the western part of **Bluffer's Park** at the time of print. It appears that the **Lake Ontario Waterfront Trail** that runs through or past the 11 parks along the bluffs will be completed. When done, it will connect 11 km of Lake Ontario waterfront with a path more accessible for all to enjoy.
• Arrive early (before 10:30 am) if you want a parking spot in **Bluffer's Park** in summertime. This is a very popular spot!
• The **Dogfish Pub** is a 20-min walk from the parking lot by **Bluffer's Park Beach** (the eastern beach). Walking to the eastern point of that beach and back to the parking lot is a 30-min walk.

Romantic mood
• The strip of land past photo #8, at lake level, would be a perfect picnic spot. Quite secluded, with the best view of the white cliff.
• Admire the boathouses from the pedestrian bridge near **Dogfish Pub**, and then have a drink on its patio overlooking the marina.

Family fun
• The remnants of the old McClain house at the eastern end of **Rosetta McClain Gardens** will feel like ancient ruins to young adventurers.
• Using the TTC system to get to **Bluffer's Park** can be tricky for parents! The walk from the stop at Kingston Rd & Brimley Rd S is 2.3 km long, which means you'll need to walk up the hill, kids in tow, at the end of the day trip. Since 2018, TTC's **175 Bluffer's Park** route (starting at **Kennedy Subway Station**) has been extending to **Bluffer's Park Beach** on weekends (Saturday, Sunday and Holidays, between 8 am and 10 pm) from May to before Thanksgiving weekend. Consult **www. ttc.ca** to confirm it is still the case.

A little extra in the area
• Check the mini-walks #48 and #49 on pages 241-242 in the last chapter **#torontourbangems**.

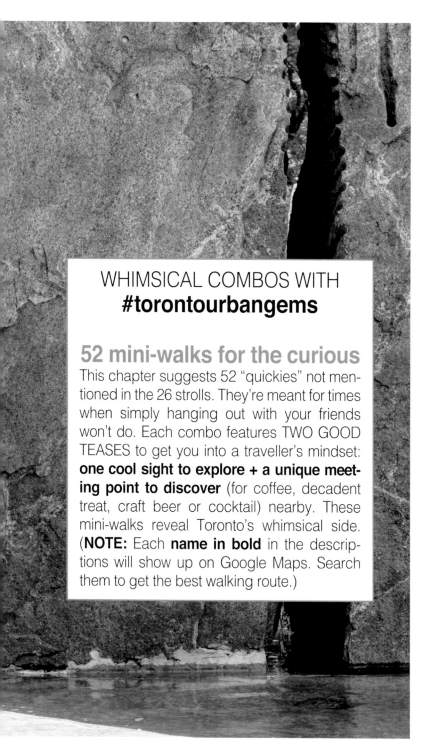

WHIMSICAL COMBOS WITH
#torontourbangems

52 mini-walks for the curious

This chapter suggests 52 "quickies" not mentioned in the 26 strolls. They're meant for times when simply hanging out with your friends won't do. Each combo features TWO GOOD TEASES to get you into a traveller's mindset: **one cool sight to explore + a unique meeting point to discover** (for coffee, decadent treat, craft beer or cocktail) nearby. These mini-walks reveal Toronto's whimsical side. (**NOTE:** Each **name in bold** in the descriptions will show up on Google Maps. Search them to get the best walking route.)

① The Upper Deck + wide cityscape
40 Avenue of the Islands, DOWNTOWN

The **Toronto Island Marina**'s bar (a 7-min walk west of Centre Island Ferry Dock on Toronto Islands) is your chance for dancing your heart out on the patio with live music while admiring the city's lights reflecting on the water. And they serve great fries too!

② Tandem Coffee + bike in a tree
368 King St E, DOWNTOWN

There's a little bike theme here, from the fun logo of a tandem bike on the window of the small café (good coffee, interesting snacks) to the mature tree which swallowed a bike in **Ray Lane** (a 5-min walk eastbound on King St E, take Bright St, and turn east into Ray Ln).

(3) George Street Diner + cathedral
129 George St, DOWNTOWN

The real thing set in the 50's, with red booths, huge apple pie on the counter, and fun details all around to take in. A 5-min walk from **St. James Cathedral** and its gorgeous stained glass windows (going southbound on George St and west on King St E).

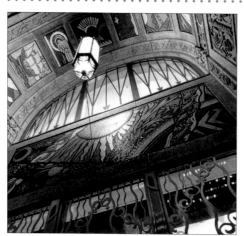

(4) Boxcar Social + Art Deco mosaic
70 Temperance St, DOWNTOWN

This gorgeous industrial café is lost in the Financial District! They serve serious alcohol and light lunch. The towering Art Deco **Concourse Building** awaits a 1-min walk away. Go check the superb mosaic at its entrance (one block south at 100 Adelaide St W).

(5) **Momofuku Noodle Bar** + dragon
190 University Ave, DOWNTOWN

Impossible to miss the *Rising* sculpture by Zhang Huan climbing up Momofuku, attached to the **Shangri-La Hotel**. The flock of silver pigeons/hands form a fascinating dragon shape you can admire before entering to enjoy Momofuku's noodles... and **Milk Bar**'s treats.

(6) **Trinity Square Café** + labyrinth
19 Trinity Square, DOWNTOWN

This café is in the **Trinity Square**, a hidden gem out the N/W door of **Eaton Centre**. The back of the old **Church of the Holy Trinity** feels like a European village! Eat homemade lunch at the social café. Enjoy the stream-like fountain. Walk through the labyrinth...

⑦ **Food trucks** + ceiling domes
100 Queen St W, DOWNTOWN

Superb **Osgoode Hall** is open to the public on weekdays (130 Queen St W). The geometric floor and ceiling domes of its central hall are breathtaking. Follow this with a classic hot-dog from **City Hall**'s food trucks next door, facing the big TORONTO landmark sign.

⑧ **Dark Horse Espresso** + artsy hub
401 Richmond St W, DOWNTOWN

Independent Dark Horse cafés all over town, including one in the basement of heritage **401 Richmond**, right across from **Spacing**, my favourite shop featuring everything about Toronto. The culture hub includes art galleries, artists and design studios.

⑨ Falcon Skybar + plane spotting
111 Prince's Blvd, DOWNTOWN

Trillium Park (off Ontario Place's parking lot) overlooks planes landing on the island and boats cruising the lake. The pedestrian bridge, linking it to the Ex grounds, faces **Hotel X** and its two spectacular bars with a view: The Nest and my ultimate favourite, The Perch (one floor above).

⑩ Barcelona Tavern + lovely carpet
@ Hanna Ave & Snooker St, DOWNTOWN

Their patio section plastered with old doors makes it a funky spot for sangria and tapas. Among many **Liberty Village** gems you'll find adjacent **West Elm** store, the intricate carpet mural (74 Fraser Ave), the covered **Liberty Market** (at Hanna Ave & E Liberty St) and more.

(11) **Roselle Desserts West** + art show
108 Dovercourt Rd, DOWNTOWN

Roselle's pastries are little edible artworks, to be followed by a visit to **Drake Hotel** and **Gladstone Hotel** (both within a 10-min westbound walk on Queen W), where art can be admired. (Note that the new owners of the Gladstone intend to carry on its legacy.)

(12) **Arabesque** + hobbit whimsy
1068 College St, DOWNTOWN

After sweet Blood Pigeon tea and baklava at Arabesque café, reach for the artisanal hut in **Dufferin Grove Park** (northbound on Gladstone Ave). It includes a **Reflexology Footpath**, a stone throw from the hut, and Toronto's only playground with mud pit.

(**13**) **Bang Bang Ice Cream** + murals
93A Ossington Ave, DOWNTOWN

Bubble waffle cones, ice cream sandwiches, home made cookies explain the long line-up in summertime in front of the small take-out counter. No sweet tooth? Try **Jimmy's Coffee** (5 Ossington Ave). Great murals to be admired on side streets and west alley.

(**14**) **Nadège** + park with a view
780 Queen St W, DOWNTOWN

Taste Nadège's amazing masterpieces, then go down the middle of adjacent **Trinity-Bellwoods Park**. Look up from the pit for a surprising view of the CN Tower. Oh, and regarding the **White Squirrel** café (907 Queen St W), yes, there are some in the park!

(15) Bar Raval + lane stroll
505 College St, DOWNTOWN

Many don't know that this unique bar in Gaudí's style, tiny but one of the most gorgeous cafés in town, serves elegant tapas in the morning. Two blocks north murals by Insect Cabaret await on **Scarfo Lane** (go northbound on Palmerston Blvd then west on Harbor St).

(16) Coffee Dak Lak + rare books
283 College St, DOWNTOWN

Their Vietnamese egg coffee is topped with a luxurious foam made of beaten egg yolk, condensed milk and strong coffee. A 3-min walk away is Postmodern **Lillian H. Smith Public Branch** (239 College St) with griffin guard, cylindrical atrium and rare children's books.

(17) Balzac's + hidden pond
@ Gould St & Bond St, DOWNTOWN

Nearby this beautiful café off pedestrian Victoria St, **Ryerson School of Image Arts** lights up at night, and **Ryerson Community Park** turns into a rink in winter. You've also got to check hidden gems in **Kerr Hall**'s courtyard across from the café (40 Gould St).

(18) Chew Chew's Diner + greenhouses
186 Carlton St, DOWNTOWN

This train-themed all-day breakfast set in the 50's offers a vast menu and generous portions (including a popular Conductor's special). On the S/W corner of Carlton & Sherbourne Streets, the historic greenhouses of **Allan Gardens** present year-round displays.

(19) ## Red Rocket Coffee + hidden art
154 Wellesley St E, DOWNTOWN

Grab a coffee at cute Red Rocket and walk north on Homewood Ave to reach **Wellesley-Magill Park** hiding a magnificent 144 foot-long water-cut steel fence by Ed Pien. A bit further, turn righ on Lourdes Ln to see **Our Lady of Lourdes Parish**, inside and out!

(20) ## Nespresso Boutique + chic park
159 Cumberland St, DOWNTOWN

This café fits Yorkville perfectly, with its slick furniture and high ceiling. And one could not imagine a better public space than nearby **Village of Yorkville Park** for this chic neighbourhood. You can also rough it up on the rooftop of **Hemingway's** (142 Cumberland St).

(21) Istanbul Café + music garden
174 Eglinton Ave E, MIDTOWN

Turkish latte with rose petals, anyone? Loved the lamps, the serving plates and the cups! Reasons enough to visit the area, but you might want to check the fun **Lois and Bram Music Garden** in **June Rowlands Park**, (a 15-min walk southbound on Mount Pleasant Rd).

(22) Bake Code + giant mouth
4910 Yonge St, NORTH YORK

Black charcoal butter croissant, anyone? This bakery with seating offers many intriguing Euro-Asian pastries. Check the Insta-ready big mouth in **Meridian Arts Centre**'s courtyard (10-min walk northbound to 5040 Yonge St) near **Mel Lastman Square** & **Cineplex Empress Walk**.

(23) Bellwoods Brewery + urban forest
20 Hafis Rd, NORTH YORK

Toronto's longest mural by Shalak Attack (on Lawrence Ave W, west of Caledonia): WOW! North of it, the gorgeous **North Park** awaits (take the stairs by the mural and go up Redberry Pkwy). The funky craft brewery is a 10-min walk south of Lawrence (take Benton Rd, then Sheffield St).

(24) Pain Perdu + a bit of countryside
736 St. Clair Ave W, MIDTOWN

Combine the best Croque Monsieur in town, from unassuming French bakery Pain Perdu, with a walk around idyllic **Wychwood Park**, a 10-min walk away. It is one of the few private streets in Toronto. (Go eastbound on St. Clair Ave W, then south on Wychwood Ave to entrance.)

(25) **Fleur du Jour** + artsy lane
603 St. Clair Ave W, **MIDTOWN**

Did you know that we can ask the City to change a lane's name? Two neighbours did such a good job of adorning the garage doors on the lane between Kenwood & Wychwood, that locals had it renamed **Art Lives Here Lane**! Combine this with some of the best French pastries in town.

(26) **Dutch Dreams** + artsy barns
36 Vaughan Rd, **MIDTOWN**

This utterly whimsical place is your excuse to share a banana split or an ice cream pancake, for an extreme sugar rush! Then take any lane westbound to reach Wychwood Ave and the old streetcar repair facility turned into the **Artscape Wychwood Barns**.

(27) **Blood Brothers** + Geary cluster
165 Geary Ave, MIDTOWN

All the underpasses off Dupont (between Christie St and Dufferin St) are adorned with murals. From **Dovercourt Rd & Geary Ave** underpass, walk west on Geary where Blood Brothers edgy branding (all over the brewery and labels of their very popular craft beers) sets the tone.

(28) **Rustle & Still Café** + Koreatown
656 Bloor St W, MIDTOWN

Purple potato latte at Rustle & Still Café and **Hodo Kwa-ja**'s walnut-shaped cakes are a good way to start exploring Koreatown. Extending from Markham St to Montrose Ave, it is dense with exotic signs and packed with tiny restaurants and shops, with vast **Christie Park** as a bonus.

(29) The Lockhart + popular wizard
1479 Dundas St W, WEST END

This combo is for Harry Potter fans! First stop at the whimsical store **Curiosa** in late afternoon (1273 Queen St W), then it's a 15-min walk for cocktails at The Lockhart: the Pensive, BetterBeer, Gin Weasly, etc. (Walk Dufferin St north to Dundas St W.)

(30) Miss Thing's + tropical break
1279 Queen St W, WEST END

Girlfriends-approved summer scenario: have dinner and cocktails (which all come in a different glass!) at this yummy Hawaiian restaurant, take the 20-min walk to enjoy **Sunnyside Beach** (westbound on Queen St W & over pedestrian bridge), and return to the tropical bar.

(31) Famous Last Words + The Junction
392 Pacific Ave, WEST END

This fun bar plays the literary theme to perfection! A funky book-inspired cocktail is just what you need after a stroll around The Junction. From cute **St Johns Rd & Dundas St W** to Annette St, it offers the best cluster of reclaimed material shops, cool restaurants, cafés and bars.

• •

(32) Pâtisserie 27 + humorous folk art
401 Jane St, WEST END

This tiny bakery serves impeccable croissants and French pastries. Then get your dose of whimsy at nearby **Roach Tackle Folk Art** (355 Jane St) before heading down Baby Point Rd to **Magwood Park** (hidden between #94 and #98) leading to Humber River.

(33) **Home Smith Bar** + flowing jazz
9 Old Mill Rd, WEST END

A very good scenario here is to combine a late afternoon walk along flowing Humber River (on the paved trail off **Étienne Brûlé Park** and back), with a drink at this castle-like bar in **Old Mill Inn**. Even better if you can time it with one of its popular live jazz evenings!

• •

(34) **The Crooked Cue** + falling devil
3056 Bloor St W, WEST END

The first time I drove by the superb door of **Our Lady of Sorrows**, I had to stop the car! Feels like something we would see in Florence, right? And just across the street is **The Crooked Cue**, a beautiful pool bar serving pub fare to share, beer, and tempting cocktails.

㉟ Birds & Beans Coffee + gazebo
2413 Lake Shore Blvd W, ETOBICOKE

Love Gordon S. Roy's art on this café with cute little patio in the back (apparently a bird watcher's meeting point). A truly lovely waterfront walk crosses three footbridges and a gazebo by the lake (a 10-min walk eastbound). It leads into **Humber Bay Park W Trail**.

㊱ Albatros Pub + peaceful waterfront
3057 Lake Shore Blvd W, ETOBICOKE

The Mimico Asylum, turned into Humber College campus, is impressive, surrounded by **Colonel Samuel Smith Park** with wetland, secluded bays, plus a skating trail in the winter. Then, uber kitschy Albatros Pub awaits, a 10-min walk away (from the S/E park exit, walk north on 13th St).

(37) **Restoration Café** + fox & beaver
2 Matilda St, EAST END

Set inside utterly laidback **Merchants' of Green Coffee** in Riverside, this hidden café is large, eclectic and unique. They make yummy savoury scones. Neighbour to one of the loveliest parkettes in town: river-themed **Joel Weeks Park**. Look for the animal sculptures!

(38) **Rooftop Bar** + memory staircase
106 Broadview Ave, EAST END

This trendy bar with cozy seating, sharing menu, and outdoor patio is nestled on the rooftop of the historic **Broadview Hotel** and offers the best East end view (and sunset)! Make sure to take the 7-storey stairs down for a bit of local history from playful artist Jennifer Ilett.

(39) **Lady Marmalade** + hidden garden
265 Broadview Ave, EAST END

Line-up a given if you show up after opening time at this famous breakfast place. The food is delicious in this narrow 2-storey restaurant cast in blond wood. Nearby tiny private **Thorogood Gardens** is open to the public (in cute Allen Ave just south of the restau-

(40) **Riverdale Perks Café** + Greektown
663 Logan Ave, EAST END

This aptly named residential café is postcard pretty and prepares delectable treats and lunch. It is located one block south of **Withrow Park**, one of the loveliest parks in Toronto, and two blocks from the effervescence of Greektown on Danforth.

41 Hailed Coffee + Seven Wonders
801 Gerrard St E, EAST END

They serve a pale and perfumed Turkish coffee in a special pot and carry delicious raspberry croissants and rose water pastries. You can then continue your travel by spotting murals of the *Seven Wonders of the World* along Gerrard and south on Broadview.

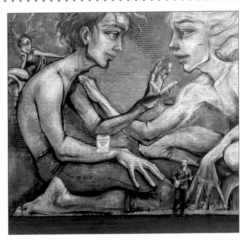

42 Surf the Greats + giant storybook
250 Carlaw Ave, EAST END

A surf mural by artist Uber5000 marks the place. Yes, people can surf around Toronto! This café with cool vibes is their hub and inside, a map points out surfing spots in the area. Don't miss the giant storybook page by int'l duo Herakut (one block west on Dundas St E).

(43) Bobbette and Belle + dollhouse
1121 Queen St E, EAST END

I come here for the scrumptious blueberry scones with clotted cream, but this elegant Leslieville bakery is all about cupcakes and macaroons, and wedding cakes. Its charming decor is fun to contrast with the over-the-top **Dollhouse** at 37 Bertmount Ave, across the street.

(44) Black Lab Brewery + dog walk
818 Eastern Ave, EAST END

The most dog-friendly bar in town, which gives it a unique ambiance! Check the gorgeous bronze tiles at N/W corner of Leslie & Lake Shore, then take the paved trail leading to **Woodbine Park** (a 5-min eastbound walk). It is home to early June's dog fest Woofstock!

(45) **Rorschach Brewing** + fountain
1001 Eastern Ave, EAST END

Here's a mini-walk featuring two watering holes: the very welcoming brewery (with fun sharing menu and cool ambiance) on Eastern Ave, and the pond with tall fountain in the middle, hidden at the heart of nearby **Woodbine Park** (with a 1-km loop trail).

(46) **Douce France** + back lanes
820 Danforth Ave, EAST END

This charming café/boutique is a genuine piece of France with croissants, chocolates, cheese, gourmet food... Check out murals around cute **Langford Parkette** just north of the café, and **The Only Café** with gypsy vibes, which has grown bigger (at 972 Danforth Ave).

(47) Castro's Lounge + beach house
2116 Queen St E, EAST END

Walking around **Leuty Lifeguard Station** along Kew Beach brings us back in time. Built in 1920, it helped save over 6,000 lives in its time. Many locals also consider Castro's Lounge a life saver! This unique bar features live music in an intimate ambi-

(48) Victorian Monkey + BC's alley
2386 Kingston Rd, SCARBOROUGH

My favourite hidden gem in Scarborough? The stretch of garage doors and fences in **Sandown Lane** generously adorned by artist BC Johnson (between Sandown Ave and Sharpe St). Fun Victorian Monkey with steampunk vibe is just south of it, on Kingston Rd.

(49) Cliffside Hearth Bread + *Passage*
3047 Kingston Rd, SCARBOROUGH

Here's a good plan! Grab hearty treats at this great bakery and walk (or drive) 1 km eastbound to the **Doris McCarthy Trail** (on Ravine Dr, off Kingston Rd). At its foot, 1 km away, look for the surprising *Passage*, erected by the water to honour artist Doris McCarthy.

(50) Mon K Patisserie + urban river
1040 Coxwell Ave, EAST YORK

Access to the staircase leading to **Taylor Creek Trail** along the stream is a 5-min walk from excellent French/Japanese bakery featuring Croque Madame, quiche and soufflé cheesecake. (Walk north on Coxwell, across O'Connor Dr, to reach **Cullan Bryant Park**.)

(51) **Broadview Espresso** + compass
817 Broadview Ave, EAST YORK

Great local café with welcoming patio and serious lattes. A 10-min walk from the **Chester Hill Lookout** overlooking the cityscape, adorned with gorgeous compass rose by artist Victor (from café, go west on Pretoria, north on Cambridge, west on Chester Hill Rd).

(52) **Aroma Espresso Bar** + rainbow
1090 Don Mills Rd, NORTH YORK

This café faces the pretty public square of **Shops at Don Mills**. It is a 20-min walk from the **Rainbow Tunnel**, a landmark first done by artist BC Johnson in the 70s. (Go south on Don Mills Rd south, east on The Donway E into Mocassin Trail Park, and keek going east.)

In 2019, I had the chance to meet a very cool group of women who found the way to organize interesting Toronto walks tailored to their needs.

I thought you might want to know how it is done so I interviewed Marilyn, the group coordinator, who initiated their adventure four years ago.

She wanted to spend time with people with whom she had a connection. She wanted to walk in good company. And she wanted to see Toronto differently, emboldened by the group.

Now what?

I asked Marilyn if she considered herself a born leader. She paused, and said: "I'm an average Type-A personality." When freshly retired from a demanding career, she looked to her girlfriend, also recently retired, and both women wondered: "Now what?"

They chose a walking tour of "art areas" that interested them both, and

found it too crowded. So Marilyn decided to ask the teacher if she would be willing to lead a private group. She was. Marilyn went into action mode.

Just ask!

This is a very important tip to take away: Don't assume. Ask.

Whenever Marilyn comes across someone who has a special take on Toronto, she simply asks them if they would be willing to lead her group.

So, when a friend gave her one of my guides, she called me to see if I would accompany them.

She has approached authors of novels set in Toronto, historians, geologists, art experts, bloggers. Some were leaders for commercial tours, some had never guided before.

I had previously organized a free walk for **Jane's Walk** (always on the first weekend of May, **www.janeswalk.com**), and one for **Historitours** (offering tours in French (**www.facebook.com/Historitours**). I loved both experiences so, of course I was in!

Start by starting

No need to plan a series of walks in advance. Make it simple. Try one to see how it goes.

Marilyn believes 20 is the perfect number of walkers. Big enough to make it affordable to cover

the costs, small enough for everyone to have a chance to talk to each other and hear the guide.

Then, she sent an email to friends, colleagues, synagogue members and gym peers stating: "I have a lady to do a walk. Interested?"

In no time, she got 40 resounding YES! responses.

It's all about you!

Wanting to accommodate her 40 friends, Marilyn opted to organize two groups, accompanying the first group on Mondays while her good friend joined the second on Wednesdays...

When Marilyn remembered that her primary goal was to enjoy her friend's company, they stopped planning two groups.

Here's another great tip for group initiators: don't forget why you started the group in the first place. It's all about you!

As the group creator, it is your job to make sure the walks are as pleasant as can be to YOU. You prefer once a month Monday morning walks? So be it.

FOR YOU AND YOUR FRIENDS

Through your lenses

Marilyn has a great tip for people she hires, who aren't professional leaders and feel a bit shy about leading a group, "Simply show us what you've researched!"

The same goes to anyone in your group who would like to lead (which would cut the fees!).

Everyone will enjoy seeing Toronto through your lenses. Find one angle (art, history, your childhood, architecture, urbanism, culture, gossip, etc.). Dig deep to uncover gems. Then share your enthusiasm.

Step by step

Through trials and mistakes, Marilyn came up with a step by step recipe to organize her yearly walking group. Want to know how she does it?

1. Decide on the number of walks. She now likes to plan 16 walks (8 in the spring and 8 in the fall).

2. Find leaders. Marilyn calls the people she is considering as guides, to ascertain if they are articulate with a voice

that projects. (She also strongly suggests they use a megaphone or other amplifying device. A must for a group of 20.)

She agrees with them on a fee and potential dates.

She asks for a short description of their walk and a little bio. (You could also ask for a picture of the destination.)

3. Plan a schedule. According to the leaders' availability... and yours, prepare a schedule with description.

4. Create a group list. Out of your circle of friends and acquaintances, prepare a group list of emails.

5. Manage a wait list. Once the group takes off, participants will tell their friends and family how much fun it is, who in turn will want to join the group.

Marilyn now has a mailing list of 200 people with no more than two degrees of separation between each participant.

6. Send your invitation. Marilyn sends her invite in January for her series starting in early spring. She allows the group one week to answer.

7. Prioritize regulars. Marilyn says it is much easier to give priority to participants who attend the whole series, and then to those who want to commit to the first 4 or last 4 walks of the season.If there are spots left, she sends a second invitation one week later.

Once someone commits (determined at the point of payment received), it is their responsibility to gift or sell their place if they can't attend, to make sure someone fills their spot. (Marilyn has noticed that the synergy is ideal in a group of 20.)

With their permission, you can contact someone on your wait list to replace them.

8. Use eTransfers. It is the easiest way to keep track of the payments, for accounting purposes. Cheques are also OK.

9. Simple rules. You will avoid complications if you stick to a NO REFUND policy and if you make the walks happen, RAIN or SHINE!

10. Specify. Two weeks prior to a planned walk, send your participants the following information:
• Walk description
• Time & place of meeting (preferably a café)
• Subway, bus, or streetcar recommendations

11. The finish line. Also specify a place to meet after the walk, for a bite and/or a drink. Ask participants to confirm so you can make reservations.

ALPHABETICAL
INDEX

How to use it

First browse through the categories listed in alphabetical order. They could help you find more easily what you are looking for: bakeries, cafés, playgrounds, restaurants, rivers, etc. Anything that does not fit into a category appears by itself in alphabetical order. Listings in italic refer to the name of artworks seen along the walks.

Montgomery's Inn
178, 179
ROM   86
Spadina House   130

N

**NEIGHBOURHOODS
(Downtown)**
Bay Street Corridor   80
Cabbagetown   96, 226
Chinatown   72, 225
Church-Wellesley   88
Corktown   16, 218
Distillery District   24
Downtown Toronto
220, 221
East Bayfront   32
Entertainment District
40, 64, 220, 221
Fashion District   64
Financial District   40,
48, 219
Garden District   226
Grange Park   72
Harbourfront   56
Kensington Market   72
Liberty Village   222
Little Italy   225
Niagara   222
St. Lawrence   24, 219
Toronto Islands   8, 218
Trinity-Bellwoods   223,
224
University   80
Upper Jarvis   227
West Don Lands   16
Yorkville   227
**NEIGHBOURHOODS
(East End)**
Leslieville   238, 239,
240
Little India   192
Playter Estates   243
Riverdale   184, 237
Riverside   236, 237,
238
The Beach   200, 241
The Danforth   192, 240
Upper Beaches   200
**NEIGHBOURHOODS
(Etobicoke)**
Mimico   235
New Toronto   235
Village of Islington
176

**NEIGHBOURHOODS
(Midtown)**
Bracondale Hill   230
Briar Hill-Belgravia   229
Casa Loma   128
Chaplin Estates   136
Davenport   231
Davisville Village   228
Deer Park   120
Forest Hill   136
Humewood   229
Koreatown   231
Moore Park   112
North Park   229
Rosedale   104, 112
South Hill   128
Wychwood   229, 230
**NEIGHBOURHOODS
(North York)**
Don Mills   243
Willowdale   228
**NEIGHBOURHOODS
(Scarborough)**
Birch Cliff   208
Cliffcrest   242
Cliffside   208, 241
**NEIGHBOURHOODS
(West End)**
Baby Point   233
Dufferin Grove   223
High Park   152
Humber Bay Shores
160
Junction Triangle   144
Little Portugal   232
Little Tibet   232
Old Mills   234
Roncesvalles   160
Swansea   168
The Junction   233
The Kingsway   234
Novotel   29

O

OCAD   74, 76
Old Don Jail   189
Old Mill Inn   234
One Old Mill   173
One York   38
Oscar Flores   28
Osgoode Hall   221
Osler Fish Warehouse   146

P

Pan-Am Games 2015   20
PARKETTES
Alexander Street Parkette   93
Baldwin Steps   130
Beaty Boulevard Park   162
George Hislop Park   93
Grafton Avenue Park   162
James Canning Gardens
93
Langford Parkette   240
Larratt Parkette   140
Market Lane Park   30
Milner Parkette   92
Nicol MacNicol Parkette
142
Palace Pier   165
Percy Park   21
Poplar Plains Parkette   133
Robert Bateman Parkette
142
Village of Yorkville Park   227
Willard Gardens Parkette
170
PARKS
Asquith Green Park   93
Barbara Hall Park   94
Bellevue Square Park   78
Berczy Park   30, 44
Bluffer's Park   212, 213
Bluffs   212
Budapest Park   167
Canoe Landing Park   69
Cathedral Bluffs Park   212
Centre Island   15
Cherry lane (High Park)   157
Chorley Park   109
Christie Park   231
Colonel Samuel Smith
Park + skating trail   235
Corktown Common   20
Cullan Bryant Park   242
David Crombie Park   29
Don River Valley Park
188, 191
Dufferin Grove Park   223
Étienne Brûlé Park
175, 234
Evergreen Brick Works
108
Forest of Remembrance
116, 125
Garden of Remembrance
116, 125

251